The Castaway's Diary

Braid Anderson

Published by YouWriteOn.com, 2010

First Edition

A CIP catalogue record for this title is available from the British
Library.

CHAPTER 1

Sungai Golok is in southern Thailand, on the border with Malaysia, and about 60km inland from the South China Sea. It is linked to Rantau Panjang in Malaysia by the Golok Bridge, built jointly by the two countries. The bridge was my entry point to Thailand. It was six o'clock in the morning when I dumped my bags off the bus from Johor Bahru. The overnight trip had taken ten and a half hours; the last six and a half with no stops for toilet, food, cigarette or anything else. I was feeling stiff and uncomfortable, having slept not a wink on the way. The young Thai man in the adjacent seat had the distressing habit of spreading his legs in all directions, like a reject from some cheap Chinese bordello.

Malaysian Immigration had been on my case, telling me 'writing books is not a good enough reason to go on living in Malaysia.' I then treated the Deputy Director to a hotel lunch in exchange for his advice and assistance. I had purchased a Malaysian shelf company and taken over a two-storey airconditioned restaurant in Johor Bahru for my wife to manage. This should entitle me to a 'Key Man' Permit, as the indispensable Managing Director of the company, but the formalities were dragging on and on.

Having visited his office six times in as many weeks, I was finally ready to submit my application, before my many-times-extended visa expired for good. Meanwhile I was leaving home at 6.15am and returning any time between 10.30pm and

12.30am. The intervening hours were spent running the restaurant, and desperately casting around for a Malaysian partner - preferably one with cash to inject. My cash reserves had dwindled alarmingly, and I'm no restaurateur.

I was a construction Project Manager for many years in Australia, Malaysia, Singapore, Indonesia and Papua New Guinea. But I always wanted to write books, and Project Management is a very full time occupation, allowing no time for such things. So I decided to 'retire' for a couple of years, and gamble on producing books which people might buy and read. Of course, I was so busy writing the books that I neglected to research how I was actually going to *sell* them. Four books finished, another two underway, and not a buyer in sight. But all is not yet lost. My *The Writer's Handbook* finally arrived after a four month wait - the week after I gave up the restaurant.

I had returned to Immigration for my final appointment with everything in order - all 611 sheets of paper, being 13 copies of 47 different forms etc. Unfortunately 'my' Deputy Director had been suddenly posted out, and his replacement professed no knowledge of my case. Except to tell me "Of course you realize it is illegal for you to be running the restaurant before your Permit comes through, and it will take more than three months to process. In the meantime we cannot renew your current visa again." A most informed statement for someone who knew nothing about my case! He could not have cared less that the lease on my house was paid for another year.

4

I handed back the restaurant to the owner of the building, forfeiting my RM20,000 deposit in the process, never mind the RM40,000 it took to set the place up. I found out shortly afterwards that the owner regretted giving me a three year lease with rollover option at my discretion, and wanted the place back. Instead of coming to discuss it with me, he talked to his friends at Immigration.

My wife could have run the restaurant standing on her head, as she has plenty of experience, and she is Singapore Eurasian, with Malaysian relatives. Which was why I got the restaurant in the first place. Unfortunately, when the Gods frown, they don't believe in half measures. My wife had suffered a stroke while in America, and was now in the Expensive Care Unit of a Florida hospital, in coma. Now I was suddenly broke, since I had already transferred all the money in the joint account into my wife's Singapore CPF account, so I couldn't spend it! At least she would be looked after when we could get her back to Singapore.

I rented out my house in Johor Bahru, and fled to Thailand 24 hours ahead of the Immigration deadline; on the principle that a change is as good as arrest. Singapore, though much closer, is far too expensive these days, and my money situation was down to rental income and little else. As I write this I am renting a flat on the top storey of a small cheap hotel. The rent is half what I receive for my house in Johor. My computer and most of my personal belongings are still in my house, and I have opened an account at the Bangkok Bank with minimum deposit. I now have bank accounts in Singapore and Thailand with next to nothing in them!

On my arrival at the Thai end of the Golok bridge I was hailed by a motorbike taxi driver. He was quite confident in his ability to convey me and my three bags. The big brown bag went on his knees, while I held briefcase in one hand, hold-all in the other. I told him I wanted to eat roti canai, so he delivered me to a Malay stall, where I ordered roti and teh tarik. Unfortunately the dahl curry was sweet, a specialty of the local Malays.

Having paid my 25p for breakfast I went in search of a cheap hotel to lay down my head. The beca driver knew just where to find what I wanted. Now I sit at the writing desk in the top room scribbling this. I'm doing it because, while poring over *The Writer's Handbook* I came across the section on National newspapers. It said that many now use freelancers, instead of filling the building with staff.

I thought, why not write something and see if they'll print it? A weekly article on my trials and tribulations - and travels - of the next few months, might enable me to stay alive, in order to write a weekly article..........Until one or other of the Great Novels is published. Then I might even manage to haul myself back to Scotland, which I haven't seen for thirty years. It's been a long, long journey.

If you are looking for a short stopover on your way from Malaysia to Bangkok, you could do worse than Sungai Golok. Just across the Golok bridge from Malaysia, it is less than an hour's drive from Kota Bharu, via airconditioned bus, cost RM2-60. There are plenty of hotels, ranging from International - at international prices - to real budget hideaways. I tend to specialise in the latter, my recent finances having excluded me from the pleasures of the more exotic.

Near the lower end of the price range are places like the Nam Thai Hotel No.2, which is where I am writing this. A large room with double bed, private shower/w.c., ceiling fan, writing desk and wardrobe will cost you 4 pounds per night, at the current rate of about 40baht to the pound. Television is an extra 50bht. They will try to tempt you by saying they receive Malaysian television.

Imagine if you will how much more vibrant and exciting British television would be, if the first five minutes of every news bulletin was devoted to a graphic blow-by-blow description of what 'The Prime Minister said/did today/yesterday'. Then decide if you want to stay in your room and watch Datuk Sri Dr. Mahatir Mohammed. He is now one of the region's Senior Statesmen, so he is free to say things like "All BBC reporters are liars and cheats. They can't help it, they're born that way."

Anyone brave or foolish enough to say the same in public about him would very soon be in big trouble. In my humble opinion from personal experience, Malays are among the most accomplished of liars and cheats anywhere, behind their oh-so-friendly smiles.

The other week I came across two different articles in the same issue of the same Malaysian newspaper; from which could be deduced that for child bashing you can be fined *no more than* RM10,000. But for printing offensive words about a rich and powerful man, you can be fined RM10,000,000!

If you must catch up with what's going on in the world, much cheaper and more enjoyable to do so via the SUN newspaper available after 10am - for 15bht over a leisurely cup of tea.

A slightly better airconditioned room at the Nam Thai costs 250bht a day, but I personally don't like airconditioning. Even in my house in Johor Bahru I chose to install ceiling fans throughout. But then, I suffer from sinus problems and you don't - do you? Other hotels with aircon as standard start around 300bht, and go right up through 1,000 and beyond. The Merlin is 400, Venice 500, then up through Parkson, Marina, Genting.

Taxis as you know them are very rare beasts in these parts. The local method of transport is by motorbike taxi. These are quite safe and reliable, and every time you turn round there will be one within hailing distance. The licensed drivers wear distinctive waistcoats - different colours for different groups - with the driver's number on the back. They also have taxi stations where squads of them await fares.

Golok is very much a motorbike society. Here you can see with your own eyes just how much it is possible to transport on a 125cc motorbike, within the compass of the driver's arms, legs, chin and the handlebars. Every morning a stream of them zip past the hotel at 50kph from the direction of the river. I would hazard a guess that some of the cargo comes across the river from Malaysia by means other than the bridge; though one would expect most of that trade to be in the other direction. Maybe farther from the bridge?

On the eastern side of the peninsula Golok is the southern terminus of the Thai rail system. Considerable quantities of freight move in and out, with much of the inward traffic being trans-shipped for onward delivery to Malaysia by road. Flanking the railway are vast timber yards, where timber from Malaysia is trans-shipped. There is a perfectly good railway bridge across the river, linking up with the Malaysian railway system. But neither Government-run organisation seems the least interested in utilising it. Instead, up to a hundred lorry loads of timber each day cross the road bridge from Malaysia, most of them unloading at the railway yards. Then Thai lorries reload it for onward delivery in Thailand! In the park on the town side of the railway line sits an old 4-6-0 steam locomotive, No.175 of Class E, built by North British Locomotive Co. of Glasgow in 1913, and withdrawn in 1970. That's not quite what the notice says. According to THAT, Springburn is in England!

At the Nam Thai the 'towkay' at the front desk is very helpful and speaks good English. This helps with the train timetable, which is all in Thai script. Passenger trains from Golok go all the way to Bangkok, with connections to the west coast of Malaysia as well. If you are browsing at the book stand on the station platform, make sure you don't forget to pay for anything you take. The owner carries an old Peacemaker revolver on his right hip, which you can't see when he's sitting

9

down.

A half hour train trip will take you to Sungai Padi. I think it's well worth the trip to see a different type of small local community, which has been almost bypassed by this century. Just make sure you don't miss your return transport - there is no decent hotel I know of.

A little over an hour by minibus - 45bht each way - takes you to the beach at Narathiwat, the State capital. The beaches are clean and safe, and Narathiwat itself is a cosmopolitan city, not much bigger than Golok. You can get there by regular passenger bus, but I don't recommend doing so, unless you have masochistic tendencies. Buses are not noted for their high safety record in this neck of the woods.

This part of southern Thailand was, until about 1902, part of a small Malay Moslem kingdom, until Thailand annexed it. There is still some well-disguised hostility towards the Thais from the local Malays. There is even a small Independence movement, which occasionally flares into violence. Things have been quiet in recent years, but I wouldn't be surprised if it rears its head again in the not-too-distant future.

Night life is varied in Golok, depending on what you want. There are plenty of bars and discos in all the larger hotels, but be careful if you are on any kind of budget. Then of course there are karaokes almost everywhere - the current *other* social disease of South East Asia.

But if you want to see how the locals like to enjoy themselves, you won't do much better than the Andaman Cafe. In spite of the name, this is one of the local nightclubs, with affordable prices. The first night I went there was talent night. Twenty six (yes 26!) local girl hopefuls take turns to sing a song each. Then they come back in threes and fours to share another song and dance routine. Most, though not all of them, are excrutiatingly bad singers. But the costumes - what there is of them - are well worth a second glance. Though I dare say they would never qualify for inclusion on Style With Elsa Klensch.

The regular singer is Lisa, who *can* sing, and will sit and have a drink and chat with you. Since she drinks Milo(!) she is not hard on the pocket, and well worth listening to. Her English is more than passably good, which is a fairly uncommon trait in Golok, outside the hotels. A large bottle of Carlsberg lager costs 80bht here, and you don't pour it yourself. By the time you are about to top up your glass, one of the waitresses will swoop on the bottle and do it for you.

Eating out can be any kind of experience you care to name. Unfortunately most of the local stall holders speak no English. I get along fairly well by speaking Malay, which many of them understand. Along one side of the street between the Merlin Hotel and the Marina is a long row of takeaway food stalls. Here you can buy all kinds of foods, including fried chicken and roast snake. The snakes are alive in a cage until you order! With the chicken it is best to order a leg, rather than breast. The local chickens are free range. Therefore they have big strong legs and not much on the chest. A whole leg of chicken at one of the Moslem stalls costs 20bht, including rice and vegetables. Be sure to ask for the vegetables or you may end up with the chicken on its own for 15bht. The extra 5 covers rice, dry fried onions, lettuce, coriander and a couple of spring onions. These stalls are open from morning until evening.

After sundown, the next street up from the Merlin is closed off for the night market. Tables and chairs are set up in the roadway, with large umbrellas and tarpaulins, and a myriad of stalls. They sell everything from snacks, through full meals, to cakes and sweetmeats. There are foods from Thailand, India, Malaysia and China on sale, including soups, noodle and rice dishes, and fried snacks of all sorts. If you look hard enough you will even find a burger stall! I prefer the little stall where the two young ladies sell spring rolls for 4bht each. The food here is all very cheap.

Slightly further up the scale are the larger Chinese-run (Yes, they're everywhere) open air restaurants. These usually have the menu printed in English as well as Thai and Chinese. Prices range from 20bht for soup, fried rice or noodles, to 50bht for a large filling portion of sweet and sour pork, beef in oyster sauce, or similar, complete with rice. At these places a large bottle of Carlsberg costs 50bht.

A cup of tea in the local coffee shop is 5 or 6bht for a cup, 9 or 10 for a large glass of teh tarik (that's the one where they pour the tea back and forth until it froths). The ubiquitous motorbike taxis are a standard 10bht from most places in town to most others. The man-powered trishaws are more expensive, but their mostly older drivers are usually more knowledgeable and obliging. Unfortunately they are a dying race, becoming more difficult to find on a casual basis.

I had been informed by Malaysian Immigration that I must stay out of the country for at least a week. My plans for the next few months after that are tenuous to say the least. My two Malay friends who run a bus ticket agency in Johor Bahru, owe me RM10,000, which is all that remains between me and starvation.

Since they don't have the money to repay me, I told them they must look after me on my return to Malaysia. The elder one - call him Adam - has a house in Pasir Puteh, Kelantan, where I intend staying, until we can find a cheap kampong house for me. In the meantime I left my tv and vcr with the other one in Johor Bahru - we'll call him Zainal. The idea is for him to sell them in order to pay for a lorry to transport my household effects - and computer - from JB to Pasir Puteh, when we find a house.

At the time I left JB - in a hurry because of my visa - Zainal did not have Adam's new address (he said). Instead, he gave me the name of the Pasir Puteh Fire Chief, who is a friend of them both. In the meantime I have rented the top flat in the hotel for a month. At least if there are problems in Pasir Puteh, I will have a roof to come back to, for a while at least. The flat is costing about RM230 per month, whereas the cheapest room is twice that on a daily basis. Hopefully, when I go to Kelantan next week, there will be somewhere for me to go TO. In the meantime I go on living out of my travel bag. At least I have some pads and pencils, so I can do some writing.

I have now discovered that in Sungai Golok it is cheaper,

13

and sometimes more pleasant, to have a beer at the shop next door. Excuse my preoccupation with the gentle art of beer drinking, but next week I will be in Kelantan. Beer in Pasir Puteh, Kelantan, is practically non-existent. The State Mentri Besar, Nik Aziz, would like to mould it in his image of Heaven. Funny how we all have different ideas on that subject. He has now banned all public dance performances - including traditional - for fear of khalwat. To an ignorant Mat Salleh this means more or less the close proximity of unmarried-to-each-other males and females of the human species. Fair joyrides are also banned for the same reason. There is a rumour around that we may soon see segregated buses!

Back to the shop in Golok, where the lady owner fancies me. Which is why I can drink my beer there for a whole 40bht per large bottle of Carlsberg. I like to mix it with a can of Sprite, to produce the Anderson Shandy. I discovered the advantages of the place two evenings ago, when it was raining heavily. She has a good awning over the pavement, sheltering a marble table and matching bench seats. The benches are surprisingly comfortable, as they have shaped backs for support. I return the cheap beer favour by buying all my cigarettes there. Krongthrip Lights at 18bht per packet of 20 are a bit of alright, and a good smoke. If you want to pay 40 to 45bht for a packet of Kent or Marlborough - made in Thailand by the same company - that's your business.

Added attractions are also available while sitting sipping my shandy at the pavement table. Including the younger lady, who sits and sews at the (made in Scotland) ancient Singer treadle sewing machine. PLus Long Tall Sally and Button Nose. These are attractive young housewives, who supplement the family income by entertaining an occasional gentleman client, of their own choosing, and at their own discretion. A rather genteel manner in which to ply the ancient trade. Button Nose keeps chatting me up, while I play with Long Tall Sally's two year old daughter. I share my beer with them, and we have a gay (is that Politically Correct?) old time. In spite of the fact that I speak not a word of their language, and they not a word of mine. Long Tall Sally is only relatively so, for an ethnic Chinese. Actually she comes up to about the bottom of my nose, and it's quite a long nose - more so by Asian standards.

The occasional gentlemen visitors are more easily conversed with, as they speak Malay. The Malaysian Chinese regular has the sometimes painful habit of poking, prodding and reading palms when he's more than two sheets to the wind. His Indian mate is a mite more reserved. They both come from Kota Bharu, across the border in Kelantan, and visit Golok just about every weekend on 'business'; to escape their wives, and enjoy a few alcoholic beverages. Bone Dome, the Chinese one, keeps telling me how we could do a real good business in girls for a 'mere' RM100,000 investment!

I simply sit there enjoying my shandy, and join in the conversation in Malay when I can. AIDS being somewhat endemic in these parts, it is inadvisable to do otherwise. And in any case prices are starting to skyrocket even here. Better just to watch the world go by, look and listen, but do not touch. Don't misunderstand me, I'm as red blooded as the next man. But surprise, surprise, I have been a most filial husband for most of my adult life. My first wife and I were both virgins when we first made love, and I didn't touch another woman until my first marriage was already in ruins 12 years later. Yeah, yeah Grandad, tell THAT one to the grandkids!

When I married, it was blessed by God, and I had visions of Happily Ever After in Heaven. That must sound excessively juvenile and naive, but it was how I felt at the time. To those who read this with incredulity, my sincere condolences. You really don't know what you're missing. When everything is common and everyday, there is no longer any real magic in anything. To be truly spellbound, and believe with all your heart, is the greatest magic of all. Sometimes self deception is a great deal more desirable and beneficial than self analysis, or expensive therapy. Why throw away a perfectly good dream for the sake of a grim reality? And pay for it to boot! Tell that to Sigmund's heirs, and listen to the excrutiating screams from the bank vaults.

That probably brings me into conflict with many child psychologists also. Why denude children of their magic illusions before absolutely necessary, thereby exposing their nudity to the bitter winds of reality, before they deserve to be so exposed? Childhood is the Age of Magic, and should forever remain so. Frankly, I've never really known many children among the hundreds I've experienced - including a busload of my own - who needed a psychologist. Mostly, where there was a real need, it lay with the parents.

Where was I? Back in Sungai Golok I trudge up to the fourth floor to write this. The old body is overdue for its next million mile service. Just doesn't seem to have the performance it had when new. But I can't afford any expensive spare parts right now, and I surely don't want to send it back to the manufacturer yet.

How can I be Mortal? – I am ME
How in all Creation can this be?
When young I was Immortal
I could stride through any portal
And the future was Forever – don't you see?

Incidentally as of nothing, I bought two sausage rolls for 9bht today. Here a sausage roll is exactly that - a sausage baked inside a bread roll.

CHAPTER 2

I went for a walk yesterday, in search of some answers on the railway bridge mystery. There had been repeated blasts of a diesel locomotive horn early in the morning, progressing as if from Thailand to Malaysia across the bridge. From the level crossing I followed the tracks riverwards. Sure enough, the inside halves of the rails were brighter than the outside, signifying that something had recently used them. I was within fifty metres of the truss girder bridge when a uniformed gentleman drew up alongside me on a motorbike. "Where are you going?" he asked in English. I explained that I thought I heard a train crossing the bridge that morning, and pointed out the brightness of the rails. He said yes, a train had crossed that morning, there was usually one a week each way. When I questioned him further he was unable to give many details, just that a few wagons were usually taken across and back. He Also told me I could not go closer, informing me that the notice I had already passed forbade it. I apologised and walked towards town, thinking what a waste of a perfectly serviceable rail line and bridge.

My money was reaching full ebb, and I didn't really want to withdraw any from the bank account. I could take out 600bht before they closed it, but I had to keep something in reserve. As things turned out I ended up at the shop next door again that evening. I had bought a packet of cigarettes there, and discovered once in the flat, that she had given me too much change. When I went downstairs, my Chinese friend was in the act of opening his first bottle of beer for the evening, so that was that. I explained my shortage of funds to no avail.

We sat and sipped to the usual sights and sounds of a Golok evening. Every so often one of the cinema advertising vans would pass by, drowning conversation. These are positively unroadworthy old utilities with large gaudy advertising hoardings mounted on the back, and LOUDspeakers. Most of the popular movies seem to feature moustacheod villains with machineguns.

The evenings are also spiced by the patrolling of the better-heeled youths on their Harley Davidson and other choppers. Some of which are way out, and make the 'Renegade's' mount look like suitable transport for frail old ladies. Talking of old ladies, there is one work-worn ancient who calls in at the shop every evening for her tot. The shop lady religiously measures the drink into the ancient's special glass. It looks like port, and smells like what it is - a local potent brandy substitute. Having downed her tot, the old lady continues on her way. She never stops to chat, simply looks around, drinks up and leaves.

I sometimes think my shop lady is into something other than shopkeeping, but not for me to pry too much. Nevertheless, it's hard to miss the money changing hands with lists of who knows what. One young man regularly receives a substantial amount in exchange for his list. He also seems to be involved with the girls of the night next door again - or should that be next-next door? One very organized and chicly dressed young lady sometimes joins us at the table, complete with cellular mobile phone. The phone rings, she chats, makes a call of her own, a motorbike appears, and off she goes.

Late last night a young man with an entourage ranging from baby to 70 years old called at the shop. He was juggling money, counting the coins in order to buy two candles, while arguing with the 70 year old, who seemed to want the money for something else. The baby in the young man's arms was crying, and since my remaining cash was not quite sufficient for another bottle, I dropped the coins in his top pocket, while shushing the baby. I then said goodnight all round and went upstairs to bed.

Earlier in the evening I seemed to be getting into a ticklish situation with the ladies. The shop owner was staking her claim to me, to the extent of telling a couple of people I'm her boyfriend! The sewing lady had come out of her shell, and was sitting beside me sipping shandy. The ladies of the night next door were starting to make some not in the least subtle remarks for my benefit. And finally the young one from the hairdressing salon on the other side of hotel reception, sat down and got into the act. She held up the fingers of one hand twice in front of my face, pointed at me, then upstairs in the direction of my flat. Since she looks all of fifteen years old, I did a pantomime of putting her over my knee and spanking her. She stood up, stamped her foot at me, and took off down the street in the huff. I hope I'm not a cradle snatcher, but in any case 1,000 baht is an exorbitant price - or was that 100? This morning when I came back from the bank it was Red Face time.

The hotel desk clerk informed me that she is 26 years old (!), and what she was signifying was that at 55 I'm not too old to have some fun upstairs. I poked my head round the end of the hotel desk and gave her a smile. She tossed her head, and proceeded to ignore me. Never mind, my week is up, and I'm off to Pasir Puteh tomorrow. I hope I can find someone when I get there. Every night at the flat, before switching off the light above my bed, I have to say goodnight to Miss Brazen. Looking up at her from the pillow before extinguishing her is really quite rude. She is sculpted in relief on the front of the lampshade. Whoever made the original mould did an excellent job. She is nude, and complete in every detail. Goodnight Miss Brazen.

On Monday morning I walked back across the Golok bridge to Malaysia, having served my one week 'banishment' in Thailand. Sunday evening had been spent drinking shandy at the shop next door, as usual. There was one amusing incident with the young ladies of the night one more door along. It can be quite educational just to watch them sometimes. They sit around in their pavement shanty, awaiting motorbike taxi pickup on behalf of clients. Or run across the street to Chonun House on demand. The real cheapies can just nip inside out of sight for a short time. Last night one of the ladies seemed unhappy with her upper endowments, and kept sticking a hand up under her tee shirt to check and adjust. Then she went into the 'changing room', and reappeared wearing a leopard-skin dress. As she exited I caught her eye, and opened the top of my shirt. Looking down inside, I held up one finger, looked on the other side, and

21

held up a second finger. I looked straight at her and held up my right thumb. All joined in the laugh, including the leopard-skin dress.

I decided to take to Kelantan only what would fit into my brown travel bag, in case I had nowhere to stay in Pasir Puteh. The flat was paid for another three weeks, just in case. Furthermore I was unsure how long a visa Malaysian Immigration would give me. The brown travel bag is now more than twenty years old. It is exactly maximum allowable airline carry-on dimensions, and I bought it prior to a trip to Indonesia in 1974. At the time I thought it was quite expensive, but it has proved its value many times over since then. It has travelled tens of thousands of miles, and visited in the region of thirty or forty countries.

At Immigration there was a young Malay woman on duty. She asked my business in Malaysia, and I gave her my best smile. I told her, in Malay, that I intended writing articles on parts of her beautiful country off the normal tourist track. She bid me a smiling welcome to Malaysia and chopped my passport. Between Immigration and Customs I took a quick look - two months! I could hardly clear Customs and head for the bus station quick enough, before someone had a change of heart.

I boarded the N0.29 air-conditioned bus to Kota Bharu via Pasir Mas, and paid my RM2-60. At Kota Bharu bus station I had a fifteen minute wait before the N0.3 aircon bus left for Pasir Puteh, cost RM2-50. Less than an hour later the bus was traversing the northern suburbs of Pasir Puteh, while I kept a lookout for the Fire Station (Balai Bomba). During a previous stay in Malaysia I had driven an Alfa Romeo Alfetta painted chili red. It was known to all and sundry as the 'kreta bomba' (fire engine).

A brand new set of buildings flashed by on the right of the bus, with the sign in front BALAI BOMBA PASIR PUTEH. But the whole place looked deserted and unoccupied. Should I get off here? Were you allowed to stop the express bus short of the bus station? Was this Balai Bomba in service or not? I sat there undecided for several minutes.

The bus was slowing down, and I made up my mind to get off if it stopped. I struggled with my travel bag from under the seat, while trying to awaken the elderly turbanned gentleman in the aisle seat. We were still entangled when the bus stopped. One passenger got off, and as the driver re-closed the door, I shouted 'nanti, nanti'. I rushed down the aisle, and the driver re-opened the door. We had overshot the fire station by at least two kilometres during my indecision, and subsequent hand-to-hand combat.

Having retraced more than half that distance in the blazing sun, I spotted a coffee shop on the corner of a side street, and decided to have a drink. The serving girl didn't really want to talk to me, and professed not to understand my query regarding the whereabouts of the Balai Bomba. However, another customer came to my rescue, explaining that what I had seen was the new Balai Bomba which was not yet in use. The current one was just two hundred metres up the side street from the coffee shop! That was where my luck temporarily ran out. At the fire station I was informed this was the boss's day off. His deputy phoned to discover that Encik Ismail was not at home. He had gone to visit his father, who lives in the kampong, and has no phone. Would I care to await developments in the coffee shop?

I sat there checking my remaining cash assets. RM15-50 in total - bus fares to Thailand and back again, plus five Ringgit!

Within half an hour Mr.Ismail turned up, having received the message from his wife when he returned home. He told me Adam was indeed in town, and drove me to his house. It was now two in the afternoon, and Adam was due to leave for Johor Bahru that evening with his family. His house there was up for sale, and there had been developments. Some of the proceeds would go towards paying the RM10,000 he currently owes me. I have previous experience of just how long such things can take in Malaysia, so I did not get my hopes up too much.

Adam's English is considerably worse than my Malay, which in turn is barely sufficient to maintain any kind of conversation. Mr.Ismail did not have a specific house for me, as Zainal had intimated. With time running out it was decided that I should stay in Adam's house until his return from Johor Bahru. That evening I waved goodbye to them all and prepared to settle into a strange house.

CHAPTER 3

I was left alone in Adam's Pasir Puteh house in the late evening. It is a two bedroom lowset concrete house, containing all his Johor Bahru belongings. I slept little that first night in a single bed with one inch thick wafer mattress. In the morning I was stiff and sore from the experience, and already yearning for my own bed. It is Queen size with interior spring mattress. This is not such a luxury as it may sound. Twenty five years ago I had a nasty accident in an Australian coal mine. For a couple of weeks afterwards I was paralyzed except for head and left arm. Three smashed vertabrae, dislocated left hip and fractured right thigh. The accident happened in late June, and it was almost Christmas before I could walk properly again.

Meanwhile I ran the opencut coal mine from my hospital bed, until I could hobble around. I insisted Matron bring me a phone I could reach with my functional left arm. My mine supervisor, foreman fitter and union shop steward all had to report to me at the hospital at least three times a week.

Nowadays the back and hip misbehave like spoiled children if they're not treated right. I limped around Adam's house until the motor parts warmed up, then went for a walk. Adam had left me RM50 and said he would be back in a few days. I walked round the neighbourhood, checking out the local minimart and coffee shop on the highway, then strolling through the rubber plantation before returning 'home'. I was barely in the door when Mr.Ismail called with his deputy Rosli and roti canai - in the red fire station minibus complete with flashing light! They chatted for half an hour before going back to business.

In the afternoon I walked to town, to see what was there, and buy an English language newspaper - it's not that far to walk is it? It was much farther than I thought, about seven kilometres in fact. Not a very bright idea on a hot sunny tropical day. By the time I reached town, and walked another kilometre or so around the streets, I was ready for a shandy, but settled for a cup of tea instead. We're in beerless Pasir Puteh now. Nowhere could I find one of the English language newspapers, *Star, Sun, or New Straits Times.*

Thunder clouds were building up not too far away, making the return hike even more daunting as I headed back. On the inward trek I had noticed taxis plying back and forth along the highway, picking up and setting down passengers, a la bus. Nothing ventured nothing gained, I waved the next one down and asked how much to Adam's place. Fifty cents! How I wished I had known that earlier, it would have saved more than fifty cents in wear and tear.

On Wednesday morning I breakfasted on roti telor and teh tarik at the coffee shop on the highway - there was no food in the house. Breakfast cost me RM1-40, cheaper than Golok. The dahl curry was not really curry, but at least it wasn't sweet like the one over the border. On my return to the house, Mr.Ismail brought a potential buyer to look at the Honda car Adam has for sale. This is one of the ways in which Adam makes a living nowadays. He brings cars from Kemaman in southern Terengganu and sells them in Pasir Puteh on commission. Unfortunately he had forgotten to tell anyone, including me, where the car keys were, so the buyer could not test it.

Thursday and Friday were spent mostly walking round the neighbourhood. I must have walked about fifteen kilometres in total, looking at houses and asking questions. One small kampong house near Adam's place is coming vacant next month. A bungalow a kilometre away is empty, but has been repossessed by the bank. Three kilometres in from the highway, behind the rubber plantations is a vacant end terrace house. But the jungle is ten feet high in front, and the vandals have been at it. Not to mention the fact that it seems to have been in regular use as a toilet. It would cost at least three months rent just to make it fit for habitation.

I washed my trousers late Friday afternoon. Though I had brought only the one pair, I had to wash them, as they were soaked with sweat from my safaris. With the wet trousers hanging on the line I then discovered I'd run out of tobacco! I have been rolling my own cigarettes from 'Bison' tobacco in order to cut down on expenses. Now I could REALLY cut down, with no trousers to go walkies! Beside the sofa I came upon some local Kelantan-grown tobacco, together with some rolls of the vegetable matter in which the poorer locals roll their own. I tried my hand at manufacturing one, lit it up, and spent the next five minutes coughing.

It rained overnight, and my trousers were wetter in the morning than when I hung them out yesterday. There was no word from Adam - his 'few days' could mean anything in Kelantan. On checking my funds, I scraped up five Ringgit, not quite enough for a packet of 'Bison'. Ho hum, thought he, sitting trouserless in the lounge, wondering if an Orang Puteh would arouse much interest walking around the streets in a borrowed sarong.

I had decided to go for broke to find a house on the beach, before remembering I am already broke. Dark clouds of depression gathered in my mind. Then Mr.Ismail - my saviour - turned up with a loaf of bread and twenty ringgit. Adam called him and said he should be back on Monday. No worries now, twenty five ringgit can last me until at least Tuesday night. I calculate on living expenses of ten ringgit a day, which is pretty close.

On Saturday afternoon I tested Adam's washing machine, which he said was not working. First thing I discovered was that the plug on his extension lead was shorted and burned inside. So I took the plug off one of the fans and used that. Then I replaced the fan plug with the base of the casserole cooker plug - which was also broken - and the top of the extension lead plug. When I switched on, the electronics seemed okay. To me it looked as if all that was required was a fitting for the inlet hose, without which nothing else would work in sequence, because there was no water to activate the water level switch. I filled the damned thing up with buckets of water, and voila, the washing machine worked.

On Sunday Mr.Ismail came to take me for a drive. He had

business to do in Bachok, which is on the coast halfway to Kota Bharu. After his business was completed we drove down the coastal road, via Kg.Rekang, Ger, Telong, Ayer Tawar, Semerak and Kg.Golok, all delightful little towns. On the way we passed the local tobacco drying kilns, and called in to see Mr.Ismail's parents at Kg.Kandis. Theirs is an old highset kampong house among coconut palms, fifty yards behind the beach. I went for a walk along the empty unspoiled stretch of golden sands, and wished there was a house for rent right here - I'd be in like Flyn.

We chatted and shared a couple of coconuts with the family, while the chickens and goats vied for scraps. The house has mains electricity, and a water well with electric pump. From the front verandah you can look through the palm trees out over the South China Sea to the offshore islands.

Ismail told me Adam was trying to get me a rebuilt Morris Minor with 1,300cc Mitsubishi engine. He thinks he can get one on the never-pay system via his contacts, to help towards what he owes me. That would suit me just fine at the moment, but I won't hold my breath waiting for it to arrive. I want a house on the beach, but Adam wants me close, where he can 'keep an eye on me'. I'll probably have to settle for a local kampong house near Adam, while I locate a beach house myself later.

Adam and family returned late on Monday, and there were lots of people in the house all evening. I gave him the messages from various callers, including the two who wanted to test the Honda. Adam told me that after the monsoon, which begins next month, he would like me to go to Kemaman with him to drive the cars back. He will give me RM100 per car when sold. It turns out that he doesn't have a driving licence! In Pasir Puteh he's okay, but on the highway in Terengganu it's only a matter of time before he's caught.

The rest of the news was no lorry, no house, no money from his JB house, not much of anything. But that's the Kelantanan way. As my father would have said 'They aye take half an hour to be five minutes'. And if you get yourself all worked up about it, trying to push them to *move*, you only end up bursting a blood vessel, while they carry on as usual. Better simply to cultivate the habit of patience, and cut whatever corners you can yourself.

On Tuesday we went for a drive in the white Honda sports car Adam had brought from Kemaman. At Bachok we had lunch at the beach, where Hamid (Adam's seven year old son) and I played boats with chunks of driftwood and coconut shells. He had the best boat - not fair!
Next stop on the drive was Adam's parents' house in a remote kampong between the ocean and the main highway. His mother makes and sells local herbal medicines. She even packages them in soluble capsules - Greenpeace colours - like antibiotics!

Following my normal habit, I took off for a walk through the countryside. The first few hundred yards of the footpath was tight going, where the jungle was re-taking control from the rubber trees. Then I broke out to the padi area, where I walked along the earth dykes, though none of the fields has water yet.

On the way I found some wild mint, which I gathered. I had discovered before that Malaysians in general don't know its uses, and therefore don't cook with it. I passed a few cattle and water buffalo, grazing contentedly, before stumbling on a smallholder's wooden house. Poor country people in Malaysia are much the same as elsewhere, most hospitable.

The family offered me sweetcorn from their own crop, which was cooked to perfection. Since I had nothing to offer in return, I demonstrated how to use the wild mint when cooking sweet potatoes. Then I went for a walk round the 'property' with four of the daughters. The youngest, aged one year, was naked in my arms, while the second youngest held my hand. The farmer has seven daughters, and still trying for a son! He keeps a few birds in cages, and has a trained monkey to climb the coconut trees and toss down the ripe coconuts. Sometimes he and the monkey hit the road on his old bicycle, and pick other people's coconuts for a small fee. I could have wandered round the padi fields all day, but Adam had sent out a search party. They found the girls and me feeding a couple of cows. Adam wanted to get back before dark, as he was not sure of the lights on the car. It had pop-up lights, and one of them wouldn't pop up. He asked me if I could have a look at it when we returned. I seem to have a reputation with Adam and Zainal for being a fixer of things which have broken.

When we returned to Adam's house I spent an hour trying to fix the pop-up headlight which wouldn't pop up. I discovered that several teeth had been stripped off the cogged wheel which raises and lowers it. The only remedy for that was a new gearwheel, which is not affordable at the moment. So I cut a length of a small tree branch and wedged it open. Adam wanted it fixed because we were driving to the beach at one o'clock in the morning to buy fresh fish from the fishermen.

It was nearer two o'clock before the first boats beached with their catch. Meanwhile we sat at one of the open air stalls selling cooked fish, and ate our fill. As soon as the first boats grounded on the beach the bargaining began in the light of pressure lamps. We ended up with five kilos of good quality fresh ikan merah for RM20. That is forty percent of the price I paid at the central market in Johor Bahru when shopping for the restaurant. The smaller cheaper fish are half that price, but Adam wanted the best tonight. I noticed some small shark on sale also, and made a mental note. I like shark, partly because there's no mucking around with bones, but also because it's good to deep fry. Not that I say no to ikan merah, which is best chopped into steaks, and has no messy small bones.

We met up with some of Adam's friends at the beach, and revisited the makeshift stall for tea and chat. This was quite boring for me, since my Malay is not the best, and the way they speak it in Kelantan is very different from Johor Bahru. Somewhat akin to Cockney versus plum-in-the-mouth English. Young Hamid and I went beachcombing with the aid of Adam's torch. The beach here was quite steep, so I had to keep a careful eye on him and the waves. An occasional larger wave would race up the steep part, and overflow onto the flatter area above, trying to catch the unwary. We found a few shells, but nothing to write home about. Shells seemed to be remarkably scarce on this particular stretch.

Following the conversation at the Tea House of the Kelantan Moon, we all crammed into the car and went visiting - at three thirty in the morning. The people Adam had been talking to were his cousins, and they had invited us back to their place in Selising for breakfast! By the time we got there it was after four o'clock, and I was supposed to go to Thailand today. The house was next to the mosque, entry gained by a gate in the mosque wall, through which the car could just squeeze with inches to spare. Part of the reason for the trip was to pick durian. Apparently early morning is the best time for this, I have no idea why. Nor do I like durian - the smell is enough to turn me off, whatever it tastes like. I tried some in Perak years ago, with a clothes peg on my nose. It tasted not bad, but even without the smell, I wouldn't walk a country mile to eat any for free.

Nevertheless I was enlisted to help with the picking, by torchlight. While we were at it, we picked a heap of mangosteens from one of the adjacent trees. I was reluctant at first, because it looked to me as if the trees belonged to the mosque. But Adam explained that his cousin shared the land with the mosque authorities. He also kept the grass cut and the weeds down, in return for which the fruit belonged to him - after the mosque's (roughly) ten percent of everything picked. Breakfast was ready at five thirty, in time for me to receive an earbashing as the mula called the Faithful to morning prayer, via the loudspeaker fifty feet away. Adam's cousin doesn't need an alarm clock to get him up in the morning. There was more chat over rice - and fish of course. By this time I was dying for a sleep, but it was not to be. Back on the highway, we headed AWAY from Pasir Puteh. I asked where we were going, and was informed that we had to pick up a batch of Mother's herbal medicines, for delivery to several bomohs. I said in that case, could we please stop at the first coffee shop with curry puffs. I explained that they were not for me, but for my 'little friends'. At the coffee shop I bought eighteen small curry puffs, which raised more eyebrows, as they wondered what army I intended feeding.

At Mum's house everyone was still bathing and getting the sleep out of their systems. As soon as I had said my hellos to everyone, I took my bag of curry puffs and headed off into the jungle. It was now light enough to see where I was going without the aid of a torch. Twenty minutes later I was at the house of the poor rice farmer with seven daughters and no sons - yet. The farmer was already out in the padi, and waved to me as I drew close. I had timed things just about right. Breakfast was not yet prepared, being served after the first hour or so in the padi. So I produced my large bag of curry puffs, and was delighted by the reception they received. It had worried me that these people had fed a complete stranger, when they had barely sufficient for themselves. I had been empty-handed that first time, except for the wild mint, which they could pick themselves.

Three hours later I was bleary-eyed on the bus to Thailand with RM100 in my pocket. I had told Adam about my back and hip, and we agreed it was better I go to Golok for the remainder of the time I had paid for.

CHAPTER 4

It was raining at Kota Bharu bus station, and I dodged in and out of cover, trying to spot the No.29 bus. Unfortunately the buses do not board at fixed spots, merely taking whatever berth is available as they arrive - all without cover from the rain. I must have missed one, because it was forty minutes before I boarded. At Rantau Panjang I made a run for Immigration, then waited fifteen minutes in the hope the rain would go away. But it had set in for a while, so I then made a dash across the bridge to Thai Immigration, where I waited a further fifteen minutes or so; by which time the rain had reduced to drizzle.

New building was taking place at my usual shortcut to the hotel, but no way was I going to go round the extra kilometre by road. I negotiated the clay mounds and plank 'bridge', to the detriment of my shoes, which were now covered with mud. At the hotel I arrived somewhat dirty, wet, and bedraggled. It's high time I bought an umbrella - so I can absent-mindedly leave it somewhere when the rain stops; as I have done with at least four already in Malaysia. The towkay's smiling welcome made me feel at least a little better, and I made my way upstairs to 'my' flat.

The cleaning lady had done a good job, and the laundry I had left behind was neatly folded on the big double bed. I said hello to Miss Brazen on the lampshade, showered, changed, and settled in. It was at this stage that I decided to try my hand at writing newspaper articles, since it may be a year or two, or

36

never, by the time I earn any income from the Great Novels. I went out and bought a couple of shorthand notebooks, consulted my diary, and started writing at six o'clock in the evening. When I checked my watch it was midnight! My stomach told me I hadn't eaten all day, so I went to the street market, bought four spring rolls for sixteen baht, and devoured them in the flat.

On Thursday I slept late, before going for a walk round town. Back at the flat I fiddled with the third article, then fussed over the new book. It is intended to be part of a series, the latest of which is already written. Now I'm going back in history to when the hero was younger. I always seem to finish up doing things back to front! Having got not far with either, I sat down and wrote some jibberish, calling it the Nuts and Dolts Department. It goes something like this:-

Once upon a time Lunatic - he's an insect from the moon - went to the doctor with a head under his lump.

"What happened?" asked Dr.Pyramid.

"I was putting on some toilet water and the seat fell down."

Dr.Pyramid gave him an obscene prescription. Lunatic, being prone to premature articulation, called the doctor a pyramidiot. Dr.Pyramid then sued Lunatic for definition of character.

On his way to court, the doctor met a colleague, Doctor Psycho.

"Hello" said Pyramid. "Wonder what he meant by that?" thought Psycho.

In court Lunatic cleared his throat and spat on the floor.

"You can't spit on the floor here!" roared Judge Godly.

"Don't worry Your Highness, it's strong enough to find its own way out."

Dr.Pyramid's lawyer explained to the court that the good doctor was viewed as a 'real asset' by his fellow practitioners.

"Only two letters too many" muttered Judge Godly.

"That's it, I'm off" said Pyramid.

"Couldn't have put it better myself" said the judge, whose brother was an Anglican bishop. HE proposed to his bride by singing 'Abide With Me' out of tune.

Judge Godly had just finished reading - in Latin - a collection of articles written for the Rome Herald by Vice Versa (who also wrote pornographic poems), entitled 'The Secret Acts of the Apostles'. His next case was an action by the R.S.P.C.A. against a Mr. Miserly Hillfarmer, whose defence was 'The Lord is my Shepherd'. Judge Godly had that morning had a discussion with his tailor, during which he asked "Tell me Mr.Goldfarb, Jew eat kosher hungry?" Goldfarb had retaliated by sewing some rosehip seeds into the seat of the judge's trousers. He was now itching for a recess.

This place gets more and more like something out of Laurel and Hardly, thought Judge Godly. The previous case had been one of attempted rape against a wealthy Yorkshireman, who had made his fortune pumping out septic tanks - where there's muck there's money. His excuse was "Suck cess, can get lonely." Having removed his contaminated trousers in his chambers, the judge stood musing over the state of the world. Does living in a disposable society mean that Society is disposable?

"Dis pose or dat pose" muttered the artist's model of a train disappearing into a tunnel; where a funnelweb spider disguised as a nurse lay in wait to stop it smoking. If at first you don't suck seed, try drier grain.

Enough with the applause already; the wax in my ears is melting, and contributing no end to global warming. Madame WHO? To sew or not to sew, that is the question. A character called Flag McAndrew, in a book by that famous author Braid Anderson (thankyou, thankyou) once said of his Chief Steward

There wis an auld steward on a boatie

Who could 'a' weel done wi' a goatee

Tae hide his curved chin

That wis the worst sin

Ever tae be let loose afloatie

I very much doubt if Flag will ever constitute a serious threat to Rabbie Burns.

Oh my Fallen Angel

I must have gone to Hell

With my flair for writing poetry

It's maybe just as well

"Shuddup, I already said you were no threat."

"So who are you kidding?"

"My nanny of course."

I decided sleep might be the best prescription. Goodnight Miss Brazen.

Friday morning was spent wrestling with The Book again, with not much more than yesterday in the way of results. Then I started reminiscing on Places I have Been. The last time I went to Papua New Guinea, the company I worked for before called me to open and run a branch office in Mount Hagen, while at the same time building a commercial complex for the Chairman of Sir Julius Chan's political party.

When I got there, the place I was supposed to resuscitate was almost in ruins. When it rained I used an umbrella while boiling water in the kitchen. The place was infested with rats and cockroaches, workshop machinery rusted solid, etc. My first week was spent just sorting out the shambles, after which I sent the boss the following fax - fortunately he was 600km away. (Rascal = criminal; Meri = local native girl, mostly with bright red teeth, gums and tongues from chewing betelnut; 'John West'= The Sardine Man, writes a weekly column in the local rag)

'Having spent a year talking to my computer in a foreign land, I decided to return to PNG for another stint. It was the bank manager who made the decision. Sent me an important looking letter, the gist of which was could we please go back to the old system where I bank with HIM? How would you be, scribbling away on the Novels of the Century, and no basket wants to buy them? No gifted talent spotters in the publishing industry any more I suppose.

Now, with the computer still in that foreign land - along with the car, which needs a few little extras like wheels and things - I sit here and talk to myself. Or bombard the boss in Lae with facetious faxes. Silly twit bought me a new you-beaut fax machine. But only because the old one went walkabout when the bandits ambushed the company truck at the pass.

Sitting here picking the splinters from my fingernails - I'd been scratching my head - when the light bulb shrieked EUREKA! I hadn't bathed yet, but I didn't think I smelled THAT bad. Anyway, since the boss was threatening to cut off my fax - or he might have said something else - I decided to lay off him for a while.

Why not annoy one of the local newspapers for a change? Why not indeed. If that John West character in the little tin can (tincan) do it, why not me? (I?, aye aye).

Went to the Squash Club on Friday night and got squashed. Ran like hell when I saw this fierce character glaring at me from the bathroom mirror Saturday morning. Two hundred yards down the road in my sarong when I woke up and decided it was a nightmare. Then the Meris started pestering me on the way back, wanting to check what was under my kilt. One look at the savage sets of teeth dripping red stuff and it was Nightmare on Elm Street time again. And I thought I was puffed from running DOWN the hill!

Made it back to the workshop/office/brothel, where the rats respectfully stood aside for me to re-enter. Head Rat already made a deal with me that the living quarters are mine - for as long as I'm actually in them and awake. In return he gets a feed of Talon-G rat bait every day. He and the kids are thriving on it. No tele yet, but who needs it? Every night there's a prizefight down in the gulley, and us nobs on the hill have a grandstand view. Then the cops come and declare it a draw, so nobody wins any money - including Simon the Bookie. I'll probably be placed in wet cement up to the ankles for that - head first. He has plenty of cement, or so he tells me. Before he said so I bought twelve tonnes of the stuff from somebody else. Now I'm only allowed to bet on the losing horses at Maryborough. Which doesn't mean a helluva lot, 'cos they're ALL losers in Maryborough.

The rascals got into the fag warehouse the other night. My security bloke called the cops, who were there in a flash - honest, cross my heart and hope to die.

The bandits took off in their ute

With the coppers in hot pursuit

(Try poetry if they won't buy my damned books), to the soundtrack of Gunfight at the OK Corral. Then something tripped the light fantastic across my roof. Thought it was Head Rat for a moment, but he was still on the telephone - I put some Talon-G there for his midnight snack. It turned out to be The Bandit They Left Behind. He tripped once too often and did a fantastic dive onto the back lawn (lawn?), before gathering his bits together and limping over the fence. Picked the same spot as the rascal who stole my blanket off the clothesline last week. HE looked like the Caped Crusader - and probably wished he was when he encountered the long steep drop on the other side of the fence.

Anyway, the fag bandit (does that sound queer?) left some of his bits behind, so my bloke and the cops scored a few packets of Cambridge each. I told the cops I would complain to the

*Council - this sort of thing does nothing for property values.
Even Head Rat agreed there.*

*It's probably time I went to bed, but Head Rat's still having
supper in there with the family. Even Col the Chief Cockroach
was complaining yesterday. Head Rat tried to eat Col's Number
Twelve wife, but turned up his nose in the end. So would you if
you could smell her. Dunno how Col puts up with her. Maybe
she has a special technique in the dark? Come to think of it, I'm
short a couple of clothes pegs - Col?*

*Better go now, got an early rise in the morning. But at least no
concrete pour tomorrow - unless Simon gets REAL nasty.'*

On Tuesday the Great Revelation came. I had been
struggling with the new book series *Young Bridges, Army
Bridges, Engineer Bridges*, sorting things out in chronological
order. In the afternoon I browsed through *The Writer's
Handbook* and came upon *The Peple's Friend*. Having been out
of the country for nearly thirty years, I'd forgotten how popular
that used to be in my neck of the woods, with its short stories
and serials. Some of them were quite long running.

The light bulb flickered on in my brain. *Bridges* could be
made into the longest running serial they ever had! Change the
main story round a little, bring in a few more main characters,
toss in a longtime baddie, add more romantic interest, develop
some of the subsidiary characters, and by the hair of my Aunt
Jessie's toupe, I have a serial which could run to a hundred
episodes - or more. Follow all of the characters right through the
decade of the '60s.

For the rest of the week I was feverishly engaged in sorting out the new outline, ongoing story lines for the various characters, the timescale and dates of major events I could remember. It would be handy to be closer to a source of historical reference mind you. I bought a large hardcover lined foolscap exercise book of 150 pages for the episodes, plus another couple of shorthand notebooks for the roughing out, and scribbled away with my new propelling pencil. For days the outside world passed by almost unnoticed.

Until on Friday evening, Mr.Kua the baldheaded Malaysian Chinese from Kota Bharu came searching to see if I was still alive. He had a new friend to introduce to me. My pleas of busy busy, and not enough money fell on deaf ears, and I was soon ensconced in my favourite position at the pavement table. The new friend was Mr.Chua, a motorbike distributor. That rang a bell in my memory. Adam had said he could source some cheap jet skis, would Mr.Chua be interested? Certainly he would, what are the details, make and model, price etc? I told him I would have to get Adam to contact him, as I am only the middle man's offsider. We exchanged names, addresses and phone numbers, and commenced serious drinking, with Mr Chua insisting he pay the rest of the evening's bill after I had paid my first one.

Saturday was a slow starter, and I was due to return to Kelantan tomorrow, as the rent on the flat was about to run out - and so was my money. I spent the morning splashing my face and wandering round in a daze. The afternoon and evening

44

were spent transferring scribbles from shorthand notebook to exercise book, in the form of *Bridges, Episode 1.*

Packing in the morning did not take long. I had left my brown travel bag in Pasir Puteh, knowing I could squeeze everything into the briefcase and holdall. The holdall is quite small and convenient. It zips along the top, and has a carrying loop across one end. Looking at it you would think it holds not much at all. But into it I can cram a change of underwear, socks, a couple of tee shirts, light trousers, washing and shaving gear, Swiss Army knife, travelling alarm clock, the leather folder in which I keep passport bankbooks and spare money(!), small torch, sewing kit, Band Aids, aspirins, and a jar of Tiger Balm. Which usually leaves a little room for a couple of other odds and sods. All in something which looks no bigger than an average lady's handbag.

On the bus to Kota Bharu it occured to me that Christmas was just over two months away. How would a living-alone orang puteh spend the Festive Season in Malay Moslem Kelantan? My life seems to be caught in limbo right now, with my wife in a coma for 5 months, and from comfortably off to broke within 2 months. The company I worked for in Papua New Guinea is struggling to survive, because the PNG Government is bankrupt, and hasn't paid for work completed two years ago. I tried to tell the Company Secretary that he had too many eggs in the Government basket, and I had good private money contracts lined up in Mount Hagen. But my contracts had to be foregone because the company couldn't afford them AND all his

45

government contracts.

He no longer works for the company, but it's too late to change things now. They have been selling assets to stay afloat. Seven times in my career I've been called on to take over major projects which were badly behind schedule/losing money etc, and turn them round. Two of them for this company in PNG. Apart from technical proficiency, my technique is really very simple:-

1) Pinpoint the main problems and devise solutions.

2) Treat your subordinates as fellow human beings, whatever their creed or colour.

3) Always encourage suggestions from those closest to particular tasks.

4) Instil pride of workmanship in even the most humble.

5) Always bear in mind that loyalty is not a one-way street.

6) Make every effort to ensure your men have what they need when they need it. In Indonesia and PNG this entails considerable forward planning, and constant chasing.

When I arrived in Pasir Puteh the house was locked, and the keys were not where Adam said he would leave them. I went for a walk, and the rain started, so I sat in the small porch with a dose of sinusitus. Five thirty came and I was *really* worried. The man in the house over the fence came home from work. His wife must have told him I'd been hanging around all afternoon, so he came across with a big screwdriver and forced a window!

I climbed in through the window, and Adam returned half an

hour later. He and family were preparing to leave for Kemaman. I waved goodbye, and settled down in the house, alone once more.

As soon as Adam and family were gone, I gathered my writing materials, notes and diary on the dining table. It was time to do some forward planning, before writing any more of the ongoing *Bridges* serial.

Prior to the restaurant and my original flight to Thailand, I had written several books, including the one which I now intend re-writing as later episodes of *Bridges*. With all I have planned, the latter looks like becoming a saga. In which case I might as well make it a real one, rather than a half-hearted effort. One of my books is *Flag McAndrew*, which is set in almost the same time period as *Bridges*. A series of 'Flag' books is planned, with the next 3 already outlined. I have now decided that Andy Bridges and 'Flag' McAndrew went to school together, and were close friends. The *Bridges* serial will follow Andy through the '60s, while the *Flag* series of books will do the same for Flag. In the latter part of the decade they will meet up once more, by which time they will both be on their way up in big business - Andy in Scotland, Flag in Sweden. They will then team up to form the nucleus of a multinational manufacturing and construction conglomerate, which will expand during the '70s. That should keep me very busy for the foreseeable future.

Meanwhile, Andy has had to leave college in Glasgow and work as a conductor on a Glasgow Corporation bus. While Flag wanders around the world as a deck apprentice on an ocean going tanker. They both have a long way to go in the next ten years.

My Big Book, as I call it, is *Target Singapore*. This is set in the early years of next century, when Singapore is starting to feel the pinch of a slowdown in prosperity and employment opportunities. The new Indonesian strongman, who has replaced the President with his own yes-man, has plans to take over Singapore, instead of allowing Singapore to virtually take over any more Indonesian islands.

He is working hand-in-glove with the Vietnamese, who have in turn formed an alliance with the Chinese and Russians. In the latter country the most recent President has been overthrown by hardliners, and the medical profession have developed strains of the HIV virus for which they also have the antidote. They are infecting Western leaders via their vice organization in Western capitals.

Unfortunately, one of their victims is the elderly President of France, who - unknown to them - has terminal cancer. He sets up the latest French nuclear submarine to blast Vietnam off the map, as his lasting memorial to friends he lost at Dien Bien Phu.

The Indonesian strongman has hired a professional assassin from Hong Kong to eliminate the Singapore President during his big election speech, immediately prior to his Indonesian troops taking over the island. His method of takeover is quite ingenious, requiring no mass invasion. And so it goes on and on.

I sketched the outline as one way of staying sane, while incarcerated in an Indonesian jail eleven years ago, having committed no crime - not unusual in Indonesia. On my release it was back to a working week of a hundred plus hours, with no time for anything but the job in hand - Project Management is like that. Until I finally made the decision to take up writing fulltime. Which has so far turned out to be a financially disastrous decision. But I'm not about to give up yet.

My other book Tropical Trial is actually my comprehensive diary from the jail. I started it on the backs of food tin labels, and any other scraps of paper I could lay hands on, before managing to procure some exercise books. It is therefore a day-by-day account of life as a prisoner in an Indonesian jail. Where beatings are commonplace, guards sell the prisoners' food, and anything can be procured for a sufficient bribe. During my time in the jail, I went on hunger strike, losing more than a third of my total body weight - and I was never fat in the first place - until I looked like a survivor of Belsen. I refused to co-operate with the jail authorities in any way, and in the end they gave up trying to browbeat me. I spent my last month of incarceration sitting in my cell, complete with typewriter, smuggled desk and stolen chair, while the guards pretended not to notice. My first five weeks had been spent with six of us jammed into a cell which the Dutch built many years ago to hold three Indonesian prisoners. So you can imagine what that was like. On second thought, I doubt the ability of most ordinary people to truly imagine what it was like. At the time, prisoners in

South America were committing suicide in protest at overcrowding, with almost as much room as us. The Indonesian prisoners next door to us had 70% of the area of the South Americans - I measured it.

Therefore my present desperate financial situation is not as terrible for me as it would be for most people. For as long as I survive, and life goes on, I will therefore continue writing. I am quite determined to make a living from it, and have already made tentative plans for when the first income is finally generated. Like a house on the beach, with sea breezes; a cheap little car for getting around; phone/fax/Internet and improvements to the computer. Or even a new computer when income is sufficient to justify it. Without our dreams, where would any of we humans be? I sometimes think that our enormous capacity for hope is, above all else, what separates us from the other animals.

Back at Adam's place in Pasir Puteh, having had my thoughts on the future of Andy, Flag and myself - not to mention my usual digression for the day - I continued with the latest episode late into the night.

CHAPTER 5

On Monday I bought a phone card and called my wife's sister in Singapore. Adam had told me last night that there was a message to ring her about my wife. The gist of the conversation was that the family wanted me to put up the money to fly her back to Singapore, complete with attendant/s and so on. It is not the easiest or cheapest operation in the world to transport a woman in a coma from Port Charlotte, Florida, U.S.A. to Singapore. I told her I had no money left, and since they are my wife's family (she has a brother and five sisters) it was about time *they* started paying for something, until I have an income once more. Besides which, I'm sure the Singapore Government would release some of my wife's CPF money for such a purpose.

It annoys me that the only time my wife's family in Singapore ever contact me is when they want something from me. Doubly annoying when I have nothing left to give, and have no option but to say no. I told her also that even if I have the money, I will require a medical report on my wife's condition at the time, and her doctors' opinion on the safety aspects of transporting her. Only then will I even consent to it taking place, never mind pay for it. Half of our savings went into her CPF account, and the rest went into the restaurant.

At Adam's house, I cleared the dining table, arranged my notebooks and pieces of paper, and proceeded to organise *Bridges Episode 2*. My sinus problem proved to be too painful, and I could not concentrate. Mr.Ismail called round at ten o'clock, so I asked him if he could give me a lift into town. He said surely, I looked grey, as if I should be in hospital! An hour after taking the Sudafed I bought at the pharmacy, the pain was gone, and I could get on with writing.

Three days later Ismail called once more, and I removed my nose from the grindstone long enough to join him in eating some pisang goreng. He asked me when I last ate, and I honestly could not remember! Over the next week I went out just once, to stock up on enough food and tobacco to last a few days. Nevertheless I did have a couple of breaks. One was when the cat was sick all over the carpet, and I had to clean it up - making myself almost vomit in the process. Then I lifted the carpet and spread it outside to catch the sun.

By the end of the following week I was writing Episode 5, which had me crying into my hanky half the day. All about the past tragedies of Sister McConochie's life. The day after that I realized I had absolutely nothing left - no money, food, tobacco, nothing! Nor did I know what day it was, until I checked the date on the wall clock against my diary. No wonder I was out of everything - Adam was already ten days late!

I looked outside, and the weather was threatening thunder at any moment. So I sat down and wrote a note to Mr.Ismail, in the form of HELP! The note was barely finished when Adam's friend in the red Honda car came to see him. I told him Adam had not returned, and he said Adam told him he would be back more than a week ago. I said me too, but he's not here yet, could you please deliver this note to Mr.Ismail on your way back to town?

An hour later the Fire Chief (Ismail) came to attend to the emergency situation. He doused the fire with food, cigarettes, and a fifty Ringgit note. Seldom have I been so relieved to see anyone as I was right then. He said Zainal had rung from Johor Bahru, with the message that he would be in Pasir Puteh in the next few days. He would then go back to JB with the lorry, which Adam is hiring locally, load my goods, and send them here.

Adam said before he left that he had a kampong house for me, but didn't say where. Probably one of the two at the far end of the road, one of which I knew from my previous wanderings and enquiries was coming vacant. Adam has even paid the first month's rent. If he keeps on at this rate, it will take less than eight years for him to repay my loan, interest-free!

At two thirty the next day - Friday - Ismail drove up to the door, and said "Okay, let's go to Tumpat."

"But I'm busy writing, and I haven't shaved."

"You sit in the house working too long. Never mind shave, just put on a shirt and we go."

He had a friend, Mr.Rusdi in the car. Being Friday - Moslem Sunday - everyone was off work.

"Where did you say we're going?" I asked in the car.

"Tumpat, can cross to Thailand by ferry, no bridge. On the way we look at interesting things, like tourist, okay Mister Braid?" It was okay by me.

We took some narrow side roads through little kampongs, until emerging onto a better B class road. Fifteen minutes later Ismail drew into the side of the road, near a Buddhist temple.

"Come and see this" said he. I followed him into the temple grounds, wondering what on earth there could be in this out-of-the-way place. Imagine my surprise when there, inside the grounds, was the largest reclining Buddha in South East Asia! The place was Kampong Berok, and the temple Wat Photivihan. The statue is gigantic, there is no other word for it. I had no idea there was such a thing in Kelantan, of all places. But it makes sense, being so close to Thailand. The local Buddhist community making it clear that they *are* Buddhists, in the midst of Moslems. Not only that, but just a few hundred yards farther along the road is another temple, with a smaller sitting Buddha - about forty feet high.

We climbed back into Mr.Ismail's car, and left the temples behind. At Tumpat we drove the wrong way through a large Customs checkpoint, but nobody seemed concerned. Ismail said this was the 'Free Trade Area' of Kelantan, where you could buy duty-free goods of all descriptions. He parked the car opposite a long row of stalls selling clothes and fabrics. I stood and watched for a while, as they haggled over the price of a bed quilt. After ten minutes of this, I told Ismail I was going walkabout.

"Okay" said he, "Maybe one hour we go back."

I wandered off through the multitude of stalls and shops, checking prices and quality. There were some really good bargains. In one shop they were offering a perfectly good pressure cooker for RM48 - that's twelve pounds Sterling! If I'd had the money I would have bought one. I spent about ten minutes in one shop which sold Thai silk products, some of which were exquisite. Farther round the block, I came across a family loading a long wheelbase Land Rover with luxury items. It had Thai number plates - I scratched my head at that one. There must be some peculiar duty or tax laws around somewhere.

Mr.Ismail caught up with me near an eating house, and suggested a meal. I said no thanks, but I would have a drink while he ate his rice and fish. The place was not exactly clean, by any stretch of the imagination. I don't mind so much eating in such a place close to home. But on a trip like this, far from a toilet I know, I rarely eat at all. I do not recommend sudden stomach cramps in such a situation. Running for the nearest toilet - if you can find one - then having to wait with legs crossed, desperately trying to suck in rather than expel. And finally being faced with the daunting task of removing trousers etc in order to defecate in a hole-in-the-ground Asian toilet. By which time it is all too often too late already. Then what to do, with no change of clothing? Reminiscent of something from Billy Connolly I think. "Ohmagawd, it's comin', it's comin', ah canna *stop* it! *Help* somebiddy, gi'es a gerden hose or *some*thin'. Mah knees canna *stand* the INtimissy!"

I bought a packet of cashew nuts to chew at the table, with my soft drink from a newly-opened bottle. When we returned to the car, Rusdi had the boot full, and still a mountain of goods on the ground. We fitted ourselves and the goods into the car piece by piece. I sat in the back, with the rest of the area stacked to the roof. I was glad to see the car had wing mirrors - no way could he see behind in the interior one.

A few miles along the road we came to Pengkalan Kubor, the end of Malaysia. We sat for a while in an empty hawker's stall, looking across the river at Tak Bai in Thailand. I thought it would be a good idea to cross here by ferry when my visa was next due for renewal. Mr.Ismail soon put paid to that thought. My visa expires the first week in December.

"That is the middle of the Monsoon. River sometimes very full, ferries cannot cross." It would be safer for me to cross over at Rantau Panjang once more. But maybe after the Monsoon, I might cross here. Tak Bai is much closer than Golok to Narathiwat, and I want to have a good look at that town, rather than a four hour glance between minibus trips.

They dropped me off at Adam's place in Pasir Puteh at 7.30pm. An hour later Adam and family returned, accompanied by Zainal from Johor Bahru. They had met up in Kemaman, where Zainal was trying to buy a forged road tax sticker for his BMW, at about forty percent of legal price. The BMW was brought to JB from Kemaman, because that's where Zainal's friend lives. He supplies cars to Zainal on the never-never. When he never never pays for a few months, he gives it back, and takes another one!

Zainal gave me his assurance that my furniture and personal effects would be in Pasir Puteh within the next week. He would just collect the money from the man in Pasir Puteh who owed him RM500, then go back with the lorry from Selising - all fixed. A week later Zainal was still in Pasir Puteh, still waiting for the man to pay up. That's Malaysia, join the club Zainal, it's only five percent of what you and Adam owe me! I asked him where's the rent for my house in JB, which his friends the tenants were due to pay two weeks ago? He said he gave it to Adam. Before I could check with Adam, they were off to the bus station, in the van Adam brought from Kemaman this time. Zainal was finally catching the bus, having given up on receiving his money this trip.

On Adam's return I asked him did he have my rent money? No, not any more. Zainal gave him it, but then had to take it back, to pay for his road tax certificate. He will send it via Giro as soon as he gets to Johor Bahru - out of the ticket agency takings! I was visibly annoyed at this news, so Adam said not to worry, he will borrow it from a friend, and give me it tomorrow. Then he told me where my 'new' house is. As I thought, it is the yellow kampong house at the rubber plantation end of the road.

Next morning I took the keys to the rumah kuning (yellow house), and had a look inside. The outside had rather put me off, but the inside was - worse! As soon as Adam gave me the five hundred, I went to the shop and bought cleaning materials. I set about cleaning the kampong house. It is a highset wooden affair with corrugated iron roof. It was full of dust and cobwebs, as well as plain dirt. There are two small bedrooms, with a dogleg open area from the front door to the left of the front bedroom, then to the right of the second one. Behind is what must be intended as the dining room, with steps down to an add-on kitchen and Asian style bathroom/toilet. The floorboards are not tongue and groove, and have gaps of up to an inch between them in places. One hole is nearly big enough to get my foot through, and there are a few more heading that way from the dry rot. The windows have no glass, just storm shutters. I walked into town and bought mosquito mesh, hinges and handles. Then walked to the timber yard two kilometres away and carried the 10ft lengths of framing timber to the house on my shoulder. Next thing was to buy light bulbs - not a single one worked. Then the water ran out, and it took me a while to figure out why. The storage tank is behind, and the ballcock doesn't work, so the owner turned off the mains valve.

Back to town again, and I bought half a dozen rush mats to cover most of the holes and gaps in the floor. I then went round the perimeter with a surface insecticide spray, and lit two mosquito coils. It took me nearly a whole day to scrub the floors with water liberally laced with bleach - I used three litres of the stuff altogether, between the floors and the bathroom/toilet. Three days later the place was at least habitable after a fashion. Unfortunately, I still had nothing to put in it. Zainal had rung from JB to say my tenants were not in the house, but had gone back home for a family problem. I asked him so what, I gave you my spare set of keys, go and check the place out, make sure my stuff is all there, and then we'll send the lorry.

A week later Zainal rang again to say there was a new padlock on the front gate and he couldn't get in. But not to worry, their friend said they should be back any day now. Meanwhile, with Adam and family in residence, I was not getting much writing done. Until Adam presented me with a small cupboard, which fitted in between the two single beds. By sitting on my bed, I could write on top of the cupboard. It was not very convenient or comfortable, but better than nothing.

Another week went by, and my tenants had still not returned. Now the November rent, payable on the 11th, was a week late. Then Adam told me that they had not paid October either. Zainal paid it himself, because they are his friends and he recommended them. He was quite sure they would be okay; now he's not so sure. Adam had organised a lorry, which was supposed to go three weeks ago, but still waiting for the tenants' return. He told Zainal he was sending the lorry next Friday, whether they were back or not. If not, he would just have to cut the padlocks. Zainal was sure they would be back.

Next Saturday Adam went to his parents' place at Bachok for the night. Zainal rang up asking to speak to him. I told him Adam was not here, better talk to me.

"The lorry is here, but I cannot get into the house, because the tenants are not back, and they have a big padlock on the security gate."

"So, get a big set of boltcutters and cut the damned thing, then buy a new padlock when you're finished."

"Oh, cannot lah, better wait for them to come back, what do you think?"

"I just told you what I think."

"Sorry lah, I already sent the lorry away."

"So why bother to ask what I think then? Better I don't say what I really think, because you wouldn't like it!" I slammed down the phone in a foul mood. That damned lorry would have to be paid for, full or empty, for the round trip from Kelantan to JB and back. I was starting to wonder if maybe Zainal was in the pay of the enemy, or what. I had explained to him as simply as possible that, by not telling me the tenants hadn't paid October, he was exposing me to be cheated. That I *had* to know that my belongings - especially my computer - were okay, and still in the house. For all I or Zainal knew, they could have been stolen and sold two months ago already. It didn't seem to sink in at all.

When Adam came back on Sunday afternoon, I told him I was going to Thailand tomorrow for a couple of days to renew my visa, then taking the train to Johor Bahru. There I would find a lorry myself, and bring my stuff to Kelantan. If the tenants had not returned I would cut the locks, stay in the house myself until I found new tenants, entering *Bridges* and the *Diary* into the computer while there.

I rang Zainal on Monday morning and told him I was on my way to Thailand, and would be in JB Thursday or Friday morning, so he had better have my money ready for me. He had been holding the RM800 proceeds from my tv/vcr for two and a half months. That was the money which was supposed to pay for the lorry to transport my goods and furniture.

60

The Monsoon had started, and the journey to Thailand was not pleasant; but at least I now had an umbrella. Adam was worried what might happen in JB if 'the gangster' found out I was back, and I told him I was past caring. I sat in the bus, staring out at the rain on the way to Rantau Panjang. Between Pasir Puteh and Kota Bharu, much of the land was flooded from the Monsoon. Things were improving a little as we gained some altitude, but still whole stretches of roadside scenery were submerged. One benefit of having the roads raised above the surrounding countryside is the absence of potholes. The raising of the road provides efficient drainage for most of the year. I used to tell young engineers working under me that the five most important things to get right when building roads are 'drainage, compaction, drainage, compaction and drainage'. It is saddening to see so many fresh graduates with fancy pieces of paper, who do not appreciate the basic rules of good flexible pavement construction, as originally practiced by that other Scotsman MacAdam - especially in this part of the world. Flexible pavements, which form 99%+ of all the roads in the world, are designed to deform and rebound under load, rather than remain rigid and break. Without good drainage, water can find its way into the sub-base of the road. Vehicles - particularly heavy lorries - deflect the pavement as their wheels pass over, causing a pumping action. Water in the sub-base cannot be compressed - you *cannot* compress water. It therefore seeks the line of least resistance, which is usually upwards through the road seal. The seal, once broken, allows more water to penetrate, and there you have the birth of another pothole. Malaysian roads in general are full of them, and still the lesson does not seem to have been learned.

Mind you, a fair part of the blame must rest with the relevant authorities. Contractors in Malaysia are not normally awarded major road contracts without paying kickbacks. Therefore, in order to make a profit, they must cut back on the quality of the construction. This is not hearsay, I've been there, done that, and been involved in the negotiations. Twenty five years ago in Indonesia was in many ways much more excusable. I used to sit down with the Provincial Director of Public Works, his deputy and engineers, and hammer out the price for the next ten kilometre stretch of road. The bargaining and haggling could sometimes last for days. When the price was finally agreed, an extra 5% was then added, for the Director and his staff. At payment time I signed for what was now 105% and received 100%. The balance was shared scrupulously among the Director, his deputy, engineers, and on down the line. This was understandable, as the salary of the Director at the time was twenty American dollars *a month*!

In Malaysia there is no such excuse. Government officials and company executives here are paid on a par with their equivalents overseas. This is not just more than the working men under them, but in most cases, many times more. A General Manager here may be paid up to twenty times as much as a labourer working for the same company. Semi skilled and 'skilled' workers in electronics factories and similar, are paid more - as much as two hundred pounds sterling a month in fact. It's called exporting jobs from the developed countries to the developing ones. Mind you, some of the people in developed countries nowadays don't want a job.

I personally experienced a classic example of this attitude in Australia a few years ago. I had spent twenty of the previous twenty four years working in Australia as a construction Project Manager. Earlier, I had applied for Australian citizenship, but was told 'don't be daft, you're British, so you're already Australian'. Later, I went to Indonesia on my first overseas project. Before leaving, I applied for an Australian passport, and was told it would take two months, better get a British one. During my second stint in Indonesia 1974/5, Gough Whitlam changed the rules. When I went to board my flight at Singapore airport, they told me I could not board, as I did not have a visa! It took me three days to sort this out at the Australian High Commission. In the end I asked one of the higher officials which flight he would like me to catch this evening. One at 8.45 went to London, the other at 9.15 to Brisbane. He told me that was entirely up to me. I then informed him that I had his name from the tag on his shirt, and I would write to the Australian Foreign Affairs Department from London, explaining why they now had to support my wife and children in Brisbane. Fifteen minutes later I had the visa.

In 1989/90 unemployment was rife in Australia. I was doing my bit to relieve the pressure by working in Malaysia. I went back for two months, visiting my sister, sons and daughters scattered around the country - literally. I started with one son in Perth, worked across to my sister's place in Victoria, up to a daughter's house in Sydney, then on to another son's house in Townsville, Queensland. Townsville has a fullblown Immigration department, so I decided to have one last go at Australian citizenship. I had been offered the position of Project Manager on the Sports Complex in Lae Papua New Guinea, for the South Pacific Games - it was running late, and the project manager ran away. Immigration told me that no matter how many years I had lived and worked in Australia, the last twelve months before application for citizenship must have been spent in continuous residence in the country. Therefore, it would be best if I declined the offer of the job in PNG, and went on the Dole for ten months. Then I could be Australian! Straight up, that is what they actually said! As punishment for working instead of going on the Dole, I have since been stripped of my Australian P.R. in spite of the fact that two of my sons have served in the Australian Army.

Meanwhile in Sungai Golok Thailand I made feverish preparations for my trip to Johor Bahru.

CHAPTER 6

The sun was shining as I walked across the bridge into Malaysia. My bus reached Pasir Mas railway station at one thirty, where I was informed there was one train a day to Johor Bahru, departing at three thirty. The ticket clerk also informed me there were no longer any trains to Rantau Panjang, the service having been cut early in the year - as I thought.

My ticket to JB second class airconditioned coach cost me RM49-50, somewhat more than I'd anticipated. Still, I had just enough to see me through until Zainal paid me my money at the JB end. I sat for a while in the station coffee shop, spinning out two cups of tea. No matter where you go, eating and drinking at railway stations and airports always seems to be about fifty percent more expensive than outside. Which would be not so bad if it was superior quality, but it never is.

I bought a tin of sweets to suck on the journey, knowing I would not sleep, as usual. In any case I wanted to record the details of the trip, especially between Kuala Kerai in Kelantan and Kuala Lipis in Pahang. There are no main roads in most of this area, the railway being the only connection with the outside world. The country is mountainous, and there are many bridges and tunnels along this stretch. Known as the East Coast Railway, construction of the line from Gemas to Tumpat was begun in 1907, and finally completed in 1931. Little more than ten years later, the Japanese ripped up 300km of the line to supply materials for the infamous Death Railway. There are nine tunnels and a multitude of bridges, including the longest in Malaysia (609m), the Guillemard Bridge across the Kelantan River outside Tanah Merah. It was 1953 before the line was reopened after the War. The railway is not only a through transport system, but a vital social necessity for most of the small towns in southern Kelantan. Every day there is a special 'market train' in each direction, which stops at every town without main road connection. Good quality (smuggled) Thailand rice is readily available on this train, with officials mostly turning a blind eye to its origins.

While I was buying my sweets at the station coffee shop, the roti stall man jostled me from behind, and placed his money in front of mine, wanting to be served in a hurry - bad manners are international these days. Five minutes later he burned his hand on the hotplate, and I enjoyed a quiet smile. Being unable to spin out the tea any longer, I found a platform seat for the remainder of the long wait. Eventually the tea worked its way downwards, and I paid a visit to the platform toilet - at a cost of twenty cents. The railway may not turn a profit, but the toilet does!

Two passenger trains transited the station in the direction of Tumpat on the South China Sea. The first one went straight through, but the second one stopped to load boxes of provisions through the carriage windows. The tracks are controlled by some gorgeous old double-acting semaphore signals. A three-arm bracket in each direction suffices for the station precincts. The arms drop about thirty degrees for caution, and sixty degrees for all clear. So in effect, each arm acts as both distant and home signal, with three glasses per spectacle plate. Pride of place on the main platform was given over to an old preserved hand-pushed inspection trolley PKR 0795. Almost as old, but still in service, was a venerable Avery goods weighing machine.

Goats and people wandered along and across the railway tracks at will, and by two thirty a considerable crowd was gathering on the platform. There must be an earlier train, I thought, since they couldn't all be waiting for the three thirty with an hour still to go. Or maybe here they report in for a long distance train as early as others do for an international airline flight?

The mileage post at the footbridge - which nobody used - reads 502.75. I presumed this to represent the kilometres from Gemas, which would be about right. There is a shorter island platform opposite the main - hence the footbridge - presumably for the now-defunct Rantau Panjang branch service.

At two forty the signalman wandered along the platform to the ground frame and pulled a few levers. Train coming? I checked all of the visible signals and none had changed. Maybe he was resetting the points from the last train to Tumpat an hour ago? The loop is used only when two trains from opposite directions are in the station at once. Otherwise trains in both directions use the main platform, with single line token exchange taking place on the platform outside the station master's office.

By three o'clock the platform was becoming really crowded, and it seemed obvious now that they were all waiting for the three thirty. Most of them had plenty of accompanying baggage, and I started to worry about crowding on the train. Seat allocation is all very professional, with exchange of information between stations along the line, so there is no confusion. Until one actually gets on the train, only to find three people allocated the same seat - it has happened to me before.

Black clouds were building up in the eastern sky, and it looked like being a race between rain and train to reach the station first. At 3.25 there were bells and pulling of levers, followed by a milling around of passengers, heralding the arrival of the train. Five minutes later there was still no sign of it. Then at 3.35 came the clarion call of a diesel locomotive horn, and at last the train came into view.

My carriage was the first on the train, next to the locomotive. I waited patiently until the pushing and shoving was over, before boarding for The Great Train Journey. By the time I found my seat in the first carriage of the train, the crowd had disappeared to the third class coaches, and we were in motion. I had an aisle seat, but the window seat was unoccupied, so I really had two for the price of one. The toddler who had made at least ten attempts to steal my umbrella on the platform was two seats away, and came to say hello. This was fine, as the umbrella was now safely in the overhead luggage rack. The seats are like airline economy class, but with much more legroom - none of the Haarlem Globetrotters would have problems. Half the seats face forward, the other half rearward, so passengers can watch the televisions installed at both ends of the carriage. When they are working that is - ours were not. The train guard made several attempts to get them working, with a weak picture at one stage. Then he lost it again, and gave up. The rest of the journey was spent blissfully television-free. The televisions in the next carriage were working perfectly.

The makeup of the train was four second class airconditioned carriages, five third class, and a buffet car. The two second class at the front of the train were going to Johor Bahru, along with the first three third class. The other two third class, and the two seconds bringing up the rear of the train, would be taken off at Gemas, and hooked onto a Kuala Lumpur bound train. At the same station, we would pick up more carriages from Kuala Lumpur to take with us to JB Or so the guard informed me; at least I think that was what he meant. The locomotive - number 24117 - was very powerful, and seemed to toy with the train. The rear bogie on my carriage was not tracking properly, as if one axle was slightly out of gauge, and every so often it set up a considerable vibration in the carriage. For the first hour we traversed relatively flat country, until the first stop at Tanah Merah. Just before the station is a large sawmill complex called Terengganu Forest Products, just to catch the unwary. The Malaysian railway system does not even enter Terengganu.

South of Tanah Merah the terrain soon became hilly, and the railway line started to snake around hills and over rivers.

The first tunnel was negotiated at 4.55pm, and transited in twenty five seconds at 60 k.p.h. The train rushed straight through three smaller stations on the way to the second and third tunnels close together seven minutes later. We then sped through Bukit Abu and Kuala Gris, prior to popping in and out of five more tunnels in the space of less than four minutes. At one stage we rushed from one tunnel, across a bridge over a deep ravine, and straight into another tunnel. At 5.20 we stopped at a small station, whose name I did not get. The short platform and nameboard were opposite the sixth carriage, with the platform about the same length as a carriage. I would have to be more alert next time. Departing passengers got down onto the trackside and walked along the ballast to the platform. The station stop was one minute only, before the loco picked up the train, accelerating very smartly. The locomotive behaved as if it could handle twenty coaches, never mind ten. From a standing start, on a rising gradient, he was doing 60kph within a minute. Eight minutes later we stopped again at Kemubu - I was on the alert this time.

I spent some time checking the quarter kilometre posts against my watch, and in spite of snaking and switchbacking track, the train was reaching over 70kph in places. Next stop was Bertam Lama. I stood at the open carriage door and looked around. There had been a station here, but they were currently ripping up the loop and demolishing the station building! The train lurched off round the bend, and all was explained. There was Bertam Baru, a new station to replace Bertam Lama.

Facing the opposite way in the loop at Bertam Baru was a mixed train, made up of four passenger cars and four long bogie freight vans. Looking closely at it, I decided this must be the 'market train', as it had all the necessary ingredients. Van doors were open, and people were milling around them. It was here that the hot axlebox on the third last carriage of our train began to play up. At 6pm we stopped in a passing loop for fifteen minutes, while the train crew drowned the axlebox in oil.

I went back to have a look, and it was quite a struggle getting through the crowded third class carriages on the way. At the errant carriage, I got down on the trackbed and smelled the hot oil and metal. I decided it would be much quicker and more convenient to return to my carriage via the lineside, rather than through the train again. Halfway back the locomotive sounded its horn and took off! I ran forward to the next carriage, where the door was still open. By which time the train was already travelling almost as fast as I could run. There was a group of men chatting in the doorway, effectively blocking it. I shouted "SKOOSA ME!" and tried to squeeze on board. One of the more alert among them grabbed my hand and pulled me on board, while the others laughed and joked.

Ten minutes later, on a left hand curve, I had a look from the step outside the door of my carriage. The hot axlebox was trailing a dense cloud of blue smoke, but the train crew didn't seem to be too worried about it. Maybe if they pretended it wasn't there, it would go away! Ten minutes after getting underway we were doing 90kph, prior to heavy braking for Gua

Musang, gateway to the National Park.

At Gua Musang there was a five minute delay, while train crew and station staff discussed the hot axlebox. Discussion over, off we went again, complete with the faulty carriage. I leaned out of the door and signalled to the driver. Jerking my thumb rearwards, I took a drag at my cigarette, and blew the smoke out in a cloud. The driver grinned, shook his open hand as if to say 'she's right mate', and opened up the throttle.

In the loop at Gua Musang was a local passenger train which we overtook. At the next station we overtook a timber and oil train. Then the rain overtook, or outflanked us, at 7.05pm. We overtook another van freight train at the next station without stopping, before pulling up at Sungai Temau. Following the usual one minute we were off again, with no more consultations on the hot axlebox, which was smoking merrily. The next stage was half an hour, before we stopped again at Padang Tengku. Fifteen minutes later we arrived at Kuala Lipis. This is a large and important station, and control point for the line to Tumpat.

There was another discussion on the smoking carriage, before the driver returned for his bag, and took off! As he passed me I waved and asked "Who's driving the train?" He laughed, and came over for a chat. Kuala Lipis is the changeover point for drivers and conductors. As for the hot axlebox, they had decided it would last out until the train reached Gemas, with the help of an occasional dousing in oil. There it could be cut out and replaced, because Gemas had plenty of spare stock. In any case the train was due to be split at

72

Gemas, and they had plenty of lines for the 'topping and tailing' to take place. That way the train would be delayed for only an extra ten minutes or so, instead of goodness knows how long if they tried to cut the carriage out anywhere else. It made sense in a way, so long as the bearing DID last until then.

I was feeling quite hungry when the travelling train hawker came along with his baskets of wares. I checked my meager funds and decided I could afford a bag of kropok (prawn crackers) and a drink of orange. I got the kropok okay, but received what the hawker called an orange in a clear plastic bag. It looked intriguing, so I said nothing. The contents of the bag consisted of two segments of the world's biggest pink-fleshed 'orange'. It looked like a giant orange, and it even tasted vaguely like orange, but I still don't know what it really was. It was accompanied by a small bag of cili sherbet, into which one dipped the 'orange' segment - a truly unique experience.

Along came my toddler friend, who refused to go to sleep. I broke off a chunk of the segment, and off she went, chuckling and showing everyone her prize. She and the rest of the family got off at the next stop, Kerambit. This was another 'shorty' platform, and it was not comfortable for them to walk along the ballast in the rain. I carried the toddler as far as the platform - and nearly missed the train once more!

Mela was another shorty, followed ten minutes later by a stop at a red signal nowhere, for whatever reason. At 10pm we drew into Jentod(spelling?), where a backpacking redheaded European girl got on and settled down in the seat nearest the

73

non-functioning television. Kuala Krau was a larger station, where I was nearly trampled by an Indian stampede. I was standing in the open doorway when seven little Indians, including two Indian maids, DIVED into the carriage, giving me no time to get out of the way. They were very wet - and in the wrong carriage. They had run to the front of the train in the rain, only to discover their carriage was the fourth one! The rain was heavy and consistent by now - good enough to keep the hot axlebox not so hot.

At ten to one in the morning we arrived at Gemas, and the fun began. Now they had to cut out the defective carriage, in addition to the normal 'topping and tailing.' Forward, and overtake another passenger train - oops, reversing again. Unhook the carriage with the hot box, forward again, reverse again, now with only four carriages. Loco unhooks and runs round. Meanwhile the train we 'overtook' left in disgust. Then our loco took the first dropped cars and put them on front of the tail end of the train. Our four cars forward, wait, sleeping car train arrives from the south, we reverse and hit with a bang. OOps, not quite right, haul off and give it another bang, so the automatic coupling wakes up. Meanwhile the unfortunate passengers from the defective carriage have been shifting their belongings to the replacement in the rain.

Our loco heads off again, probably to stick the bad carriage in a corner with a dunce's cap. Finally, after fifty minutes, we are underway once more. Twenty five minutes farther is Segamat, a busy town in northern Johor. Then the driver decides to make up lost time. Straight out of Segamat, the throttle is wide open on level track, and within five minutes we are doing a genuine 100kph. It may be coincidence that the main road runs parallel to the railway tracks for several miles south of Segamat. We were overtaking everything on the road, with the throttle wide open for the next half hour, until the stop at Labis. After that, there was no stop for fifty minutes, though we did slow down to exchange single line tokens a couple of times. I didn't envy the men on the platforms, who received a token on a loop in their arms at 30kph! 4.25 was Kulai, last stop before Johor Bahru, where we arrived ten minutes early, at four fifty in the morning.

I wandered out of Johor Bahru railway station, and did a few bends and stretches to get the motor warmed up. Next thing was to have a cigarette in the station forecourt, before lugging my heavy briefcase, umbrella and holdall to the bus station. The briefcase was heavy because it contained so much paperwork. My notes alone were more than 40,000 words' worth - or was that the Longfellow? Let's not start those capers, I'm too tired.

At the bus station the roti stall was open for business, thank goodness. I sat down and ordered roti telor and teh tarik. Zainal's ticket agency opens at 7am, so I had a long wait ahead of me. It turned out to be longer than I thought. Zainal's brother opened the door at 7 o'clock right enough, but Zainal would be in later. He came at 8.30, and proceeded to make out he was very busy for the first half hour. Then he came through to the office with pen and paper. He said my tenants had returned while I was in Thailand, and had paid the rent. On the paper he wrote down rent plus tv/vcr, less electricity, less four hundred for the lorry which came for nothing. I was left with not enough to pay another lorry to take my stuff to Kelantan. But I had covered that before I left. Adam said he could borrow the lorry money from a friend, so go ahead and get it.

Zainal was a different person from the one I used to know. Now he behaved like a 'big boss', with not enough time to talk to anyone, including me. Nor did he have time to run me home in his car - which I fixed when it broke down on the road to Malacca. Also, he said he had lost my tenants' mobile phone number, so I didn't know if they were at home or not. He could not have been less helpful if he tried.

Before leaving, I reminded him that the receipt for the overdue loan of RM10,000 was signed by him, and if he continued to be 'too busy' to help me, I would get a lawyer to sue. Then he would have no job at which to be too busy. I can't do that of course, because I have no money for the lawyer, and things like that take literally years in the courts here. But I thought it worth making the threat anyway.

At my house in Taman Johor Jaya, the gate was locked and the doors and curtains closed. I carted my briefcase etcetera half a kilometre to the coffee shop run by my Chinese friend's sister, and explained where I had been, and what doing. The Indian provision shop owner wanted to know the same - and the video shop proprietor, and the Chinese medicine shop owner. It was about fifteen minutes before I could talk to my friend's sister and ask her what she could rustle up for me in the way of a good hearty soup. I drank tea while waiting for the 'special' to be ready. And special it surely was - the most gigantic bowl of meat and vegetable soup I have ever seen served to a single person! For half an hour I tried manfully to eat it all, but was defeated after three quarters of the way down. Nevertheless, the cook's husband thought it a magnificent effort - his wife had bet I couldn't eat more than half.

On the way back to my house, I phoned the agency, and told Zainal he had better 'find' my tenants' mobile phone number and tell them I'm waiting outside the house to talk to them. For more than an hour I sat outside the house, on the culvert wing wall, waiting patiently, until they finally turned up. They ushered me inside, and made me a cup of Ovaltine, while I explained the purpose of my journey. That until earlier this week, they had been late on two consecutive payments, and I wanted to find out what was going on. Now that I was here, I wanted to stay in the house for at least a week, while I entered my articles and serial so far into the computer, print them out, and get them off to Britain.

This was perfectly okay with them. They were very sorry about what had happened, not being able to remove my belongings and so on. They are really quite nice people, but they had helped cause me a lot of strife, discomfort, and worry. If they had said no to my request, I would have given them notice there and then, and found another tenant. But they admitted their mistake, and did their best to make me welcome, which smoothed my feathers.

The house was full of furniture, and I asked where was my stuff? It was in the master bedroom - they were using the second one - crammed in there and the back (servant's) room. I located the computer, printer etc and scratched my head over where to set it up. In the end, we put the bookcases *on top* of the desks (sometimes it pays to have 12ft ceilings), and I squeezed in between my dining table and the wall next to the door. There was enough room left to put a mattress on the floor, half under the table, where I could sleep.

At five o'clock I started typing into the computer, in spite of the fact I hadn't slept for thirty six hours. Tiredness was forgotten in the desire to get things done at last. All evening the lady of the house fed me tea, Ovaltine and biscuits, to keep me going. They invited me to come out and watch television, but I said thanks, but no way Jose, it's fifteen or sixteen hours a day at the computer for the next few days at least. I managed to enter, edit and print *Bridges Episode 1* before the eyelids kept wanting to shut. That was enough, so I went to sleep.

CHAPTER 7

On Saturday morning my tenants said they were going to Kuala Lumpur for a week, maybe more. They gave me a set of keys, and left me in possession of my house, for which they had just paid the rent! That gave me a chance to rearrange the furniture sufficient to assemble my bed. I could always change it again if they came back before I left. Tonight should be my most comfortable night's sleep in a long time - hi, bed.

I took time out to do some shopping, for tea, milk and noodles. The balance of the day and evening produced *Bridges 2 and 3* complete and printed. On Sunday I started early, and finished late, producing *Bridges 4, 5* and *6*, plus *Diary 1* and *2*. By Tuesday noon I had completed 10 *Bridges* episodes, 5 *Diary* entries, and a covering letter to an agent in Edinburgh. I printed out copies of the short synopses of my 4 books, plus my personal C.V. - both of which were already in the computer - stuck the lot in a large envelope, and drove the Mini van to the post office. The Mini is okay for short trips like this, but overheats if I drive it for much more than half an hour.

The lady at Pos Malaysia didn't like my staples on the envelope, and asked me to remove them, in stilted English. I told her in Malay that if I did that, she would have to give me some sellotape to seal it. She asked what was inside, and I rattled it all off in rapid Malay. That brought a small cheer from the other customers - I'd been rehearsing it, just in case she asked! The blonde (Canadian Irish?) lady near the back of the queue said "Wow!" and held up her thumb with a grin. I bowed to her in appreciation, and there were smiles all over the post office - most unusual.

I went to see my Chinese friend Cheetah - the one whose sister runs the coffee shop - in order to borrow a telephone handset. He was moping around the house, and brightened up no end when he saw me at the door. Having lost his job, he was hard up, which made two of us. But he had lent me RM250 just before I left JB at a time when I really needed it. I told him to follow me to my house, where I plugged in the handset and rang Adam in Kelantan. Was he sure he could still pay for the lorry? Yes he was. That enabled me to repay the RM250, and make my friend's day. Adam said my Indonesian friend Franky had rung him, asking where I was. I had tried to contact him before leaving Kelantan for Thailand, but his restaurant owner friend said he went back to Indonesia. On the second attempt I managed to raise him on his mobile phone, and he said he would pick me up at ten in the morning.

It may seem peculiar that I was able to plug in a telephone handset at my house. What happened was that before I left JB I took the handset and the bill to Telekom, and told them I was leaving soon, and would like it disconnected. The lady said okay, pay the outstanding RM350, and write down your forwarding address. I asked why she wanted a forwarding address, and she said that was to send my refund cheque in *three months* time. I begged her pardon and asked why. That's Telekom policy says she. I asked why once more, to which she answered it just was.

All foreigners in Malaysia have to pay a RM1,000 security deposit before they will connect the phone. In other words, they currently owed me RM650, but they wanted me to pay them RM350 now, while they held onto my RM1,000 for another three months. Nice work if you can get it. I asked her to give me back the handset, and it was her turn to ask why. Because in that case I'll use it until the day I leave, and get my friend to bring it back, along with my forwarding address. I might as well have the convenience, and increase the bill while I'm at it, so you don't owe me so much!

I explained this slowly and carefully to Zainal when I left. He promptly took the handset back and demanded the refund now. They told him no way, I would have to go to K.L. if I wanted it early. Unfortunately Zainal 'forgot' to tell me any of this until the other day. Meanwhile he had sent the handset to Kelantan on the RM400-for-nothing lorry, and it was now at Adam's house! If you want something well and truly screwed up, just ask the right Malay to do it for you. When he told me, I was aghast. Now, in addition to the worry over the rent, I wondered if my tenants had plugged in and run up a gynormous bill. Fortunately, when they stacked all my furniture in the master bedroom, they blocked access to the phone cable, which they didn't know was still connected.

Franky picked me up on time next morning, in the restaurant owner's car. We sat in the restaurant for five hours! My local Indian provision shop owner had asked me for advice, as he was setting up a restaurant in the heart of JB with his brother. They will be selling Nasi Padang, and I told him I could get him a Nasi Padang cook and helper from *The* original Padang in Sumatra. That was the first topic, since Franky is the labour supply agent.

We talked about what to do with my company. I sent a letter to the Company Secretary, telling him I can't afford to pay him at the moment, try putting the company up for sale, and see what reactions he gets. Adam said he has a friend in Kuala Lumpur who can get us in on the Bakun Dam project as a supplier, but I can't wait forever. If it goes ahead, Franky would be an important part of the set up.

Wednesday afternoon until Friday evening I spent roughing out *Bridges* Episodes 11 & 12. Franky turned up with his Indonesian partner on Friday evening, and we discussed a few things. They have three hundred Indonesian workers - skilled, semi-skilled and unskilled - sitting over there waiting for work in Malaysia.

Saturday and Sunday were spent entering bits and pieces, dialogue, ideas etc in the computer under *Bridges.ser*. On Sunday evening I rang Adam and told him I would go and find a lorry tomorrow, to load Tuesday, arrive Pasir Puteh Wednesday morning - make sure he had the money ready to pay. I could almost see his raised eyebrows as I said what I *was* going to do, as if it was already done.

Monday morning it rained until lunch time, when I took a cab to Taman Pelangi, where there is a transport company that plies between Kelantan and Singapore/Johor Bahru. Within five minutes of walking through the door the lorry was arranged for nine o'clock in the morning. I went back to the house, and packed up the computer, printer etc, dismantled my bed, and rearranged the furniture. In the lounge I had to shift some of my tenant's furniture to allow passage for my stuff. Then I sat down and watched television - for the first time in I don't remember how long. That became boring after twenty minutes, so I got out my pad and pencil, and did some more scribbling. I disconnected the battery on the Mini and Cheetah promised to keep an eye on it.

When the lorry arrived half an hour late on Tuesday, it was raining once more. There were just the driver and offsider, and they asked where were my friends to help. I pointed at the offsider, which didn't please them overmuch. The driver stayed under cover in the back of the lorry, while his offsider stayed in the house, with me carrying from the house to the lorry - which the driver refused to reverse in the gate. Too narrow he said, which almost prompted me to jump in the cab and show him it wasn't. But better not do that, or they might do *no* work at all. The only time they ventured into the rain was to help with the refrigerator, which one man could not handle. Even then, it was the two of them on one end, and me on the other. By the time everything was loaded I was soaked to the skin, dirty and tired. 3 beds, lounge suite, 2 bedroom suites, dining room suite, kitchen table and chairs, refrigerator, washing machine, television, computer, FIVE book cases (I read a lot!), 2 desks, a dozen boxes of books, all my modelling paraphernalia - I'm a railway modelling nut - 2 packing cases of clothing, plus fan, crockery and cutlery, and so on and on. It was an 8-ton lorry, and there wasn't much room left inside.

I waved bye-bye to the hard workers and collapsed - after stripping off my soaking wet clothes and having a hot shower. That would be my last hot shower for goodness knows how long - kampong houses are not noted for hot water facilities. Even this house had none until I installed it 3 years ago. I was the first person to live in the house after it was built. The Singapore lady owner was most pleased when I took it on 2 year lease with rollover option. When I returned from Papua New Guinea a year ago, I took up the option, and paid the 2 years in advance. Now it is my lifejacket - the rent I receive is my only source of income, until and unless I sell some of my writing. They pay me RM500 a month, and I pay the kampong house in Kelantan RM100 a month, which leaves RM400 to live on. Which is not so bad, except that ink cartridges for the printer are RM60 a pop, and postal charges are not getting any cheaper.

I had reserved a seat on the *Transnational* bus to Pasir Puteh, leaving JB at 8.30pm. At five thirty I wrote a note to my tenants, saying the keys are at Cheetah's house; did a last check round, and said goodbye once more to my beautiful wee hoose. The garden was a garbage dump when I moved in. Having removed the broken timber, lumps of concrete, glass etc, I planted bougainvillea, portulaca, some pink and purple local plants, and a curry leaf tree. The curry leaf tree was a seedling when I planted it. Now I have to keep pruning it so I can reach the top - I've asked the tenants to continue doing so in my absence, but I don't think they're very interested in gardening.

At the bus station I checked my reservation and paid for the ticket, before going to the Rasa Sayang Hotel, in search of my wife's Uncle Buang, who is the gardener there. He had just finished work, and we met at the hole in the fence shortcut. Once upon a time, when I was very busy, I would go to the hotel and book in for a few days, and nobody knew where I was. The room would be booked in Uncle Buang's name, and that was what appeared in the Register. So not even the desk clerk knew I was there, and could not tell anyone. Only the manager, myself and Buang were in on the secret.

We went into the hotel lounge and spent more than an hour catching up on each other's news. From there we took a cab to the Tropical Inn, where I had an omelette, and two glasses of beer. I couldn't resist the latter, especially when Buang said he would pay. No more beer now until the next time I go to Thailand, some time in January. Which reminds me, it is now only two weeks to Christmas.

I gave Uncle Buang Adam's address and phone number, as the kampong house doesn't have a postal address. He waved goodbye to me at the bus station, and I was off to Kelantan.

I sat in the bus pondering the latest crossroads in my life, reminiscing about Liz.

In January 1982 - when I was a big businessman - a couple of American companies sponsored me to the once-every-six-years Con Expo in Houston Texas. They paid my airline ticket and got me a Lifetime visa for the States while they were at it. On the approach to Houston airport in the Continental DC10, the pilot didn't seem too sure of himself, alternately boosting and throttling back the engines; suddenly dropping the port wing, then lifting it again, causing me to grab the seat arms. We hit the runway with a bang, bouncing three times before settling down to stay. As we taxied to the terminal, the chief Hostie announced on the public address system "Ladies and gentlemen, we have just bounced into Houston International airport."

After the show we flew to Atlanta where we were picked up by company executive turboprop and flown to Charleston West Virginia; where Liz declined to accompany me on my inspection of opencut coalmines in Arctic conditions. Then off to the factory in Gainesville Florida to view the manufacturing facilities - where a large sign outside declared

'WELCOME BRAID & LIZ ANDERSON FROM BRISBANE AUSTRALIA'

The company guest house was all ours, with a coloured housekeeper to see to our needs. It was situated at the local country club, and had its own large swimming pool, plus almost anything else you could think of. The television screen covered most of one wall of the lounge, with controls built into the settee arms. Our bedroom was as big as some people's houses, with

86

one whole wall of glass. A bit public for sleeping I thought, until the housekeeper demonstrated the bedside controls for the window drapes hidden in the wall.

The ensuite bathroom was like something out of a Roman villa, except the Romans didn't have a jacuzzi in their walk-down-the-steps bath. Didn't we have some fun in that! The decor of the bathroom was all black marble and chrome. The finale to our visit with the Americans was a fistful of tickets to Disneyworld in Orlando, with free suite at the Travelodge - and a company-paid hire car in which to drive there. 'Just drop it off at Miami airport before you go to New Orleans'. Which brings me to another diversion.

In New Orleans we stayed at the Ramada Inn, converted from the original coaching inn just round the corner from Bourbon Street. The original stagecoach entry doors were still intact, leading into the central courtyard, surrounded by colonnaded walkways outside the rooms.

For the first full day I insisted on dragging Liz to - and eating in - the local jazz haunts. All she wanted to do was find a country and western place - in New Orleans! On day 2 she donned her Gilley's T-shirt with a determined look on her face. I decided that discretion being the better part of valour, it was time to submit to the inevitable. She bought the T-shirt *'Lookin' for love at Gilley's'* at the original Gilley's in Pasadena Texas, where they filmed 'Urban Cowboy', or 'Saturday Night Cowboy', I can never remember which. She had quite a collection of originals, and some not so original at one time. *'I got lei'd in Hawaii'*, *'I only sleep with the best'*, *'I'm broke'*(for shopping), and one for daughter Gina, which read *'My Mom went to Puerto Vallarta Mexico and all I got was this lousy T-shirt'.* We took her to Hawaii next trip - where a designer fashion shop owner tried to persuade Mom to stay and work for her as a model! I thought models were supposed to be tall, but she said my little Liz was perfect for her designs.

Meanwhile back in New Orleans, I had managed to locate a country and western joint. The band was in full swing when we entered; but as soon as the leader spotted Liz's T-shirt, he held up his hands, then pointed. The music stopped dead, and resumed with 'Lookin' for love.....'
In Denver Liz experienced her first snowfall. We were supposed to spend an hour and a half on the ground before flying on to Mexico via El Paso. But the blizzard interfered with people's plans, making everyone miserable and bad tempered. Everyone that is except Liz, who was captivated by it - and captivating in her Little Red Riding Hood outfit. We went for a short drive, at the end of which Liz became an expert snowball thrower - I have it on film hitting the camera lens!

Back at the airport bar we sat next to a window, gazing at the whiteout. I ordered a couple of beers from the barman, who said
"I'll have to see her I.D."
"Pardon?" I knew what was on his mind, since this was not by any means the first time.
"I'll have to see the lady's I.D. before I can pour her a beer."

88

"You want to see my wife's I.D.? Okay."

I conveyed the message to Liz with a shrug of resignation. She strode across to the bar with her little chin leading. Drawing herself up to her full height of four feet ten, she slapped her passport on the bar, under the barman's nose.

"Is that my face? You see how old I am? This is the third time this week. What's wrong with you people, are all American women big and old and ugly, or what?"

She then strode back to the table without awaiting an answer from the barman, who was in any case temporarily speechless. He poured the second beer, then handed me a rose from the vase on the bar.

"Uh, could you give this to your lovely lady wife with my compliments sir." He was rewarded with a stomp of a children's size 5 Liz foot, while the rose flew through the air over her right shoulder to the accompaniment of

"Huh, it's half dead already, like his American women!"................

The bus trip back to Pasir Puteh was long and uncomfortable, as usual. Made worse by the fact that I had a large ulcer on my back, which finally burst on the bus. It had been building up for three weeks, a symptom of the way I had been living. Hopefully, with a house of my own things would improve. The worst thing in Pasir Puteh has been my inability to sleep, which ran my motor right out of fuel. Now I have my own bed again.

The bus dropped me off at the road into Adam's house at

5.45am. I didn't want to wake anyone at that hour of the morning, so I sat at one of the stone tables outside the coffee shop on the highway. At 6.15 a local school teacher on his way to work joined me at the table. He wanted to eat breakfast at the coffee shop before going to work in town on his motorbike. At 6.30 there were stirrings within, and a light came on. I could see what looked like the lorry with my furniture, parked outside the minimart. It was my lorry alright, but the driver and offsider were fast asleep in the cab. I walked to Adam's house, where there was no sign of life. Leaving my briefcase in the porch, I walked back to the coffee shop, which was now open, and joined my new schoolteacher friend at one of the inside tables. The roti telor and teh tarik tasted better than usual after my long sleepless night. The schoolteacher ate a large plate of rice and fish, followed by two raw eggs, broken into a bowl, and laced with soy sauce.

Having finished my breakfast, I was about to check on the lorry driver once more, when Adam turned up. He had seen my briefcase in the porch, and guessed I would be here. One of his friends joined us at the table, and we chatted, while I had another cup of tea. By the time we left, the lorry driver had woken up, and driven inside the kampong road. The lorry was parked outside my little yellow house, so the 'mud map' I gave them in Johor Bahru must have been pretty clear. Once more it was a case of Muggins doing most of the work. The lorry got within a few feet of the front steps, and the driver handed things down to the offsider, who stacked them on the raised concrete landing - no handrail - outside the front door. I carried everything inside, and sorted it out. Adam had gone to take his son to school, and arrived back just in time to miss out on the work. Except for the refrigerator, which he and I then carried inside to the 'kitchen'.

Adam said he was waiting for the money to come through at the bank at ten o'clock - it was now 9.30. The lorry driver and his mate seemed upset at having to wait. I don't know why, because lounging around seems to be what they are best at. It then transpired that Adam was RM300 short to pay the lorry, so I had to come up with the difference. Which left me with exactly RM40, broke again. Stupid old me for opening my mouth to say I had RM300+, when Adam already said he could raise the money for the lorry - what a coincidence on the amount he is short! Never mind, the rent from my JB house was due once more. I just hoped that for the first time, they would not be too late paying, after our talk on the subject. It was due on Monday, and Christmas is now just 12 days away.

I set about assembling my bed in the first bedroom, which is only just big enough to squeeze in the bed and one of the smaller wardrobes. Then began the long task of unpacking and sorting out everything else, which took the rest of the week in fits and starts. First thing - after my bed - was the computer and two desks inside the front door. Add a couple of bookcases and chairs, and that area was full - it's that size of house. After considerable juggling I managed to fit two single beds and the other small wardrobe into the second bedroom. The back room, under the bare corrugated iron had to fill in as storage area for everything I could not fit in anywhere else. But this was to be my model railway room, at which Adam laughed. There was no way I could erect my model railway in there! But my baseboards are made in the form of plywood 'boxes' with 100mm deep frames. They are all a standard 1200mm long by 500mm, 600mm and 700mm wide, in 3 pairs. I made up end pieces, side pieces and 'lids', so that they can be assembled as crates, with the scenery facing inwards, and the models, wrapped in newspaper, packed inside the frames before the lids go on. Guess who's done this before?

With a week to Christmas - and no rent from JB yet - I cleared an area big enough to erect the first two boards. Then crammed as much stuff under them as I could get, to make room for the next boards, and so on. The top surface is 1,050mm above the floor, meaning anything under 950mm high and 650mm deep can fit underneath. Last comes my special arrangement. The fronts of the boards have strips of velcro, from which my azure blue curtains hang to within an inch of the floor, hiding everything from view. In JB the layout was 6.5metres long, which is the length of the main lounge. Here I have had to make it into a 'dogleg' round two sides of the room. At one end is the station, and at the other, the distillery. The main line storage yard is behind the distillery, with trains emerging through a bridge in the backscene. I started wiring the tracks, ignoring the monsoon rains teeming down outside.

On Wednesday 20th December I wrote and posted an

92

angry letter to my tenants. Once more the rent was late - by 9 days so far this time. Which is not amusing, as I have literally no money or food left in the house. Fortunately Jussoff from Restoran Kita in town came calling that afternoon. He said he would bring me some capati and curry at midnight, on his way home.

I have to keep nearly everything in the fridge, as there are rats in the attic. Adam gave me some strong rat glue, since they are not allowed to sell rat poison here - in case they poison each other instead! I spread the gooey stuff in a cardboard box, and caught three smaller rats the first night. Initially I thought this was a good thing. But the glue catches them up, and they take a long, long time to die. Not even rats deserve to die that way, so I have now baited a large trap, which I found under the house. It is strong enough to break a rat's neck, and if not, I can hit him on the head with the hammer! At least it's quick.

I also have a number of other uninvited house guests in the form of frogs. I tried throwing them out, but they just laugh at me. Especially Freddie, whom I'm sure I threw out at least five times before giving up. I kept telling him that if he wanted to stay here, he would have to pay rent. Not only did he ignore that, but he told his mates he had found a cushie billet. So now I just talk to them, and tell them to stay out from under my feet. One unfortunate didn't heed the warning, and was squashed on the kitchen steps in the dark. I buried him in the garbage bag, pretending it was a body bag.

I also talk to the cow sometimes. Actually, he's a bull,

owned by the Imam at the local mosque, but he's very docile. The area between the house and the road was very overgrown, and the bull passes by every day on the end of his rope. I hailed the boy one day, and pointed to my weeds. Now the bull spends a couple of hours eating them every morning. Occasionally I give him a slice of bread - when I have enough for myself as well! The first day I did that he was shy to begin. I sat down on the concrete steps and waited for him to come for the bread roll I was offering. That was a mistake. He came over, and was very friendly - while slobbering all over my trousers!

My friend Ahmad across the road is a bomoh (medicine man) who keeps chickens and ducks. The ducks wander around outside most of the day, and they also help to keep down the weeds a little, though they're much fussier about what they eat. I buy a few eggs from him now and again, and we went into town the other day in his little old 1970 Toyota. His wife is the cook at one of the Primary schools, so we had free lunch, before business. One of the security men at the school had a stroke, and is immobilised on the right side, from waist down. Each day Ahmad gives his leg a half hour massage. Some of the kids were getting quite cheeky, until Ahmad told them I was the new English teacher!

At the house I had been lucky with the weather in the first few days. That was when I washed everything - and I mean *every*thing. All of the bedding, towels, clothes etc had been packed away in boxes for more than three months, and were not smelling sweet. My washing machine was on the go almost nonstop for three days, while I rotated things on the clotheslines, taking in whatever was dry, as soon as it dried. Just as well I did, since the monsoon returned with a vengeance on Sunday, and has hardly let up since. But at least my shoes are safe.

When the monsoon first started, I was in Adam's house, with him away for a few days at his parents' place with the family. He must have known something I didn't, because that was the first flood. The water in his yard rose to a couple of feet deep in the middle of the night, and invaded the kitchen to a depth of six inches. Another two inches and it would have been in the lounge, where I had already lifted the carpets. Fortunately it didn't rise any higher. What I had forgotten was that my shoes were on the front porch. Being waterproof BATAs, they had sailed away in the night, leaving me with only a pair of thongs to wear, until I bought a cheap pair in Thailand. It is taboo here to wear shoes in the house, all footwear being removed at the door. Which might be a good idea in some other countries. It really gets up my nose when I see people in (mostly) American television 'soaps' putting their boots and shoes up on the sofa or bed!

As I write this with Christmas the day after tomorrow, the rain is absolutely bucketing down. Inside the house is as dark as night, with the storm shutters closed (no glass in the windows!). My tenants finally paid the rent yesterday, so I now have food for Christmas, if nothing else. They say the Monsoon finishes by mid January, and I hope they're right. Going anywhere at the moment is an adventure. The road bridge to Bachok is gone, so Adam can't get through to his parents' house. Several other bridges are also closed, so it looks as if I picked exactly the right time to bring my belongings from JB. Right now it would be doubtful if the lorry would get through.

CHAPTER 8

Since the first heavy rain, I have had to rearrange the furniture in my little yellow kampong house, in deference to the holes in the roof. Fortunately I don't have to put down receptacles for the water, as the house is self draining - via the holes in the floors! One leak misses my bed by a foot, which is lucky, because there isn't much room in there to shift the bed. Under that one I've put my colander, to minimise splash effect.

By moving the cooker hard up against the front of the kitchen sink, it is now out of the rain. But to use the sink I have to move the cooker when the rain stops. The leak in the front room misses my computer desk by inches, and will have to be watched closely in case it 'creeps'. But that's no problem, as the computer is where I spend most of my time - as long as the electricity's on deck. When not writing, I play Solitaire, design model railway layouts, and even a few 'might-have-been' locomotives, based on Reid's Atlantic and Glen classes of the old North British Railway. On the assumption that at the time of The Grouping in 1923, the Scottish railways got together to form one group. This was actually planned at the time, but fell through because of financial constraints.

The North British also designed, but did not build, a 2-8-0 and 0-8-0 based on the Atlantic, so I'm not so far away from what might have been. Had they built the 2-8-0 in time, it might well have been multiplied for the R.O.D. as well as, or instead of, Robinson's Great Central design. They shared a similar specification, but the N.B. one had a larger diameter boiler. Chalmers' post-Great War 3-cylinder version would have been a very impressive machine, but again never built. I've also designed a 2-6-4t version of the Glen. Again, not so far away from what might have been. Gresley's later V1 class 2-6-2t for the L.N.E.R. started off with the intention of using the Glen boiler, which was a good steamer. I have even designed a 4-4-4 + 4-4-4 express Garrat, based on two Atlantic engines and a new large-diameter boiler. THAT could have been a winner in real life, given the Garrat's inherent stability. And it would probably have handled the Edinburgh-Aberdeen expresses more successfully than any of Gresley's later designs, master designer though he was. Mine is designed with an automatic stoker from the start, as many of the larger British Pacifics should have been, but never were.

Talking of Pacifics, McIntosh of the Caledonian designed one before he retired, a few years before the Grouping........ In my opinion one of the best - and least appreciated - of all the old Scottish companies' designs was the River class by Smith for the Highland. Never used by them, and sold to the Caledonian; who should have multiplied and improved it, but for the fact it originated on the Highland. It would certainly have a place on my Scottish National Railway layout; which will remain a pipedream, as I have not the skills necessary to make the models from scratch. It pains me to say so, but it's true - witness the boxes of unconstructed and half-constructed whitemetal kits languishing in the cupboard. I have successfully built a Glen,

Scott, D33, C16, Ben, Jumbo and Barney, but only just. Maybe one day I'll be rich enough to commission a top modeller to make my designs for me. Come to think of it, I can't be that bad, after building the ones I have......

The rain has *stopped* - almost - and the cocks are crowing all over the place as if it's daybreak, at 3 o'clock in the afternoon. I look outside at the lake surrounding my (highset) house, and the road which looks more like a burn in spate; and decide it's not yet time to wade to the shop.......The road has poked its head above the water, and an elderly turbaned gentleman has just said good day to me through the open storm shutter, while leaving his brown cow for a feed on my weeds - it seems to be catching on. I wonder if the brown cow and 'my' black bull will get on if they meet on the weed patch?

Ahmad's eldest son is wandering around outside - probably checking if any of the ducks have drowned. Ahmad keeps him at home to look after the livestock, because he's rather simple. But he's a nice enough young man, and very obliging. He showed me his 'shortcut' through the rubber plantation to the wood yard when I was looking for timber for the mozzie mesh. His shortcut was actually a long way round, but at least it was cool under the rubber trees, rather than out in the blazing sun - that was before the monsoon hit.

My visa is due for renewal on 23rd January, by which time the monsoon should be over. After that I intend moving to the beach. During one of our drives in Adam's car I noticed a concrete lowset house in a recreation area. Alongside the beachfront road, it is about fifty metres from the water, separated only by palm trees and sand. I got Mr.Ismail to make enquiries in my absence - my face would cost more - and he said it will be coming vacant after the monsoon, probably February. The rent is RM130 a month, or 33 pounds Sterling - I don't have a pound sign on my keyboard, excuse me.

Mr.Ismail came to see me the other day, to say goodbye for a while. He has been posted to Kuala Lumpur as Firefighting Training Officer. That's what he gets for being good at his job. Now he won't be occupying the brand new fire station. It is perfectly fit to be used, but has to await a political bigwig for the official opening - prior to which they are not allowed to use it, or so I'm told. Right now I'm off to the shop while the rain's not looking.

During a lull in the rain on Christmas Eve, I ran to the shop and treated myself to a bar of chocolate. Then I sat down and wrote a little Christmas story with a moral.

THE LITTLE PINK PORCELAINE LADY

The little pink porcelaine lady stood all alone at one end of the shelf in the shop window. It was late at night on 23rd December, and the street light outside the shop had failed. She didn't have a proper name, but liked to think of herself as Grace. When the shopkeeper had put her in the middle of the window 9 months ago, she had been full of hope that she would find a nice home. But no one had fallen in love with her, and now she was banished to the end of the second bottom shelf. Christmas was going to be so lonely, with nobody to love or be loved by. Never mind, Jesus didn't have it too easy either. He was born in a manger, so maybe she wasn't so badly off after all. The thought cheered her up for a short while, but she was afraid of the dark, and jumped at every noise.

She could see and hear the thunderstorm coming for fifteen minutes before it arrived. Mother Goose had told her there was really nothing to be afraid of, but she found it hard to believe. Now Mother Goose was gone, sold a month ago, and she had no friends left.

Grace nearly jumped off the shelf when the thunder cracked overhead, to be followed by a heavy downpour. Lightning flashed periodically, casting a momentary surrealistic light on all around, before the thunder followed. She began to tremble, and tears ran down her face. It wasn't fair for her to be so alone, cold and afraid. If only some nice person would give her a good home, she would be SO happy, and she would never misbehave.

The tears ran down her face, and onto her beautiful pink crinoline dress, and she didn't even notice. She had been so proud of the dress when she first saw it, but just occasionally she wished she could have another one to change into. The salty water from her eyes worked its way down to the price tag, on which the gum was not too strong.

At first the shopkeeper had offered her for fifty pounds, which she had personally thought was a bargain. But there had been no takers, and he had gradually reduced her price, until it now stood at twenty pounds. And still nobody wanted her. She had begun to wonder if there was something wrong with her. Maybe she didn't smile enough, or maybe there was something wrong with the back of her dress - it was so annoying not having a mirror to check things out. No REAL lady should ever be without one. Was that why nobody wanted her - because she wasn't a real lady? The thought made her cry even more.

Suddenly a light flashed in her face, and she was startled almost enough to fall over once more. She could hear voices outside the shop, and hoped they weren't burglars. Or maybe that was the wrong wish - at least burglars might find a home for her.

It was the police patrol; two bobbies on foot checking the premises.

"Hey Jim, come and have a look at this," said a voice, as the light continued to dazzle her eyes. "Look, yon wee china lady is crying!"

"Dinna be daft Bob - have you been at the bottle?"

"But she is, come and look for yourself. I've heard of such things - religious statues that bleed and so on. Maybe this is the same thing. It's Christmas after all, just the right time for it."

"It's probably the roof leakin'. Came awa', we've got better things to do than look at china figures cryin."

Grace heaved a sigh of relief as they walked away, with the younger one still arguing. That had been close, she really ought to control her emotions better. Meanwhile the price tag slowly slid down her dress to the shelf, with the ink running on the

102

twenty pounds, so it could no longer be easily deciphered.

In the morning the shopkeeper was ill, and his niece opened the shop late. It was really annoying to have been called at such short notice, but she loved her uncle, and it was Christmas Eve. At 11 o'clock a large black car drew up outside the shop. The lady inside was quite excited, pointing to Grace and talking to the driver, who looked like a banker. He shrugged his shoulders, switched off the ignition, and they entered the shop. Grace's heart was fluttering - she was sure it was her they were interested in. The man asked to see her, and the shopkeeper's niece fetched Grace from the shelf.

She could hardly control her emotions once more, as the lady gave a small squeal of pleasure. "Oh Percy" she said "She's exactly what I need to go with my Dragoon on the mantelpiece. How much is she?" asked the lady. The shopkeeper's niece was unfamiliar with the prices, and couldn't find a tag anywhere on the dress. Grace willed her to look on the shelf, which she did. But then she had trouble reading the blurred ink of the twenty pounds. However, she was an adventurous sort of girl, so she decided to have a stab in the dark.

"I think she's two hundred pounds madame."

Grace drew in her breath sharply. You silly girl, she thought, there goes my hope of getting out of here. But she was wrong. "There, I told you she was special Percy. Can't I always pick them?" said the lady.

Two hours later Grace, the little pink porcelaine lady, stood proudly on the mantelpiece of the house on the hill, beside

George, the handsome Dragoon Guard, in his dress uniform. He was so handsome, and she was so happy watching the family prepare for Christmas………

At ten to midnight on Christmas Eve my friend Yussuff from Restoran Kita turned up to wish me a Merry Christmas. He brought capati which I could not eat, because by then I had dysentery. I don't know whether it was the chocolate I had treated myself to, which tasted suspiciously stale; or the water I forgot to boil when making the milk for my tea from milk powder. Whichever, it surely gave me a king size bout of the trots. Yussuff said I should go to the hospital, and I explained that if I could stay away from the toilet long enough to go to the hospital, I would already be well on the way to being cured!

I will just have to follow my own prescription, which I have found to work in the past. That is to stop eating until it's over. That way you don't feed the bug, but drink plenty of fluid in the meantime - boiled water only please. All of which meant I could eat nothing on Christmas day - and a Merry Christmas to you Mr Anderson.

There is not even a Christian church of any denomination within long hiking distance. I love pointing out to locals that at least one of their Government Ministers - who was at one time Director of Islamic Education at the Education Ministry - was awarded his Ph.D (Syariah) at St.Andrews University in my home town. Try gaining a Doctor of Divinity at a Moslem university!

This has been a good year for seeing the home town - mostly on other people's televisions - with the British Open and the Dunhill World Cup of Golf televised here. My great grandfathers James Braid and Jamie Anderson won the Open eight times between them, with great uncle Willie taking the US Open 3 times. Muggins gave up the game at the age of seventeen - having been *made* to play since childhood - after fluking a 78 on the Old Course! Hasn't Muggins lived to regret that rebellious decision - there was no money in the game then.

One of my relations - I think the term is great uncle - was 'Tip' Anderson, one of the most famous caddies of them all. He caddied to presidents, film stars, the lot. I myself was a course steward at the 1956 Open, when my uncle Dave beat Frank Stranahan to the cut. From memory that was the year PeterThomson won his third Open on the way to equalling my great grandfather's record of five wins. Old 'Tip' had a stock of good stories.....

One day - in the off season - a Texas billionaire came for a round of golf, with Tip as his caddy. Looking around on the first tee, the Texan noticed some building work going on opposite the club house.

"What they buildin' there caddy?"

"Oh, that's the new Grand Hotel sir. Solid sandstone, and only started a year ago. They say another year or so and it should be finished."

"How high's it gonna be?"

"About seven stories ah believe sir."

"Goddam, back in Texas fifty stories, finished in 6 months."

"Goodness me, is that so sir?"

"Anyway, what's the par for this hole?" asked the Texan.

"This is a par four sir, par four."

"Goddam, in Texas this would be a par 2 - just a drive and a putt."

"Ah well you see sir, you have to watch out for the Swilcan Burn. That's a stream that crosses the fairway this side o' the green. It's four feet deep wi' concreted sides."

"Huh!" grunted the Texan, hitting a tremendous power drive, straight at the pin. One mighty bounce off the road, and into the Swilcan Burn it went.

Five minutes later the Texan was sitting on the bank, removing his socks and shoes. There was only a trickle of water, and he could see his ball close to the far side. He lowered himself to a patch of wet sand, and stood scratching his head, while pondering his predicament. Finally he decided it wasn't even worth rescuing the ball, and held up his hand for Tip to give him a boost out of the burn. Tip calmly placed a putter in the hand and said "Now for one helluva putt."

Three hours later, while leaving the eighteenth green the Texan paid Tip his fee.

"Listen Caddy, I'd like to go play a round at North Berwick tomorrow. Would you like to come along as my caddy?"

"Oh aye sir, I think I could manage that. Things are a bit quiet and ah dinna have a bookin' for the morn."

Next morning bright and early they set off in the Texan's hired

Jaguar. In order to get to North Berwick they had to first cross the Firth of Forth by car ferry. Along the way Tip listened in polite silence to tales of how all the biggest, best and fastest things belonged in Texas. When they arrived at North Queensferry, there was a wait for the next ferry. The Texan got out to stretch his legs, and gazed up in wonder at the Forth Railway Bridge, most massive steel structure in the world.

"Goddam Caddy, what in hell is THAT?"

Tip poked his head out of the car window, looked around with a puzzled expression and said

"Ah dinna ken sir, it wisna there last week!"

Meanwhile, back in Pasir Puteh I was writing The Little Pink Porcelaine Lady, between visits to the toilet. This was one of the little stories I made up for some of my first batch of kids when they were toddlers. Now they have kids of their own going to school, and the way things are progressing I'll be a great grandfather within ten years. My first child was born in 1960, and the last (so far) in 1984. Which reminds me of a local tale. When asked whether she had any children, a local eighty-year-old spinster replied "Belum" which means "not yet".

For a few months there was an advertisement running in the *STAR* newspaper here, for a Vitamin E beauty cream. Manufactured by Colonial Dames Inc of America, and distributed by Good Meat (M) Sdn Bhd!

On the night of Christmas Eve/morning, I was up all night with a very bad dose of the runs, accompanied by quite violent stomach cramps. I had finished Entry 27, but that was as much

107

as I could manage. About 3pm on Christmas Day I lay down in bed, feeling decidedly dizzy. At about 4.30 somebody knocking at the door woke me. By the time I shook the sleep from my head, got some clothes on, and staggered to the door, whoever it was had gone.

At midday on Tuesday I was well enough to go to town and post *Diary* 6 - 27(!), and *Bridges* 11 & 12 on their way to the Agent in Edinburgh. I got his name from 'The Writer's Handbook'. Hopefully he is still in business, and even more hopefully he will drop me a line before hunger gets the better of me.

While in town I bought a cheap wok and some fresh vegetables to keep me going. The balance of Tuesday and Wednesday was spent finishing and printing *Bridges* 13. About 6 times a day the 3 mosques within earshot compete with each other in calling the Faithful to prayer. Thank goodness the muezin at the nearest one happens to have the most musical voice. The second closest one usually manages to sound as if he is dying noisily in great pain. In the immediate area of the kampong there are 5 mosques, one coffee shop, and one minimart, which gives a fair idea of local priorities.

I have taken to eating curry and rice regularly, my principal regret being that my curry leaf tree is in my garden in JB and the leaves are not easy to find on sale here. One small tin of beef or mutton curry serves as the base. 2 or 3 large onions, a substantial carrot, a few potatoes, eggplant, a couple of large cilis, 2 dessert spoons of curry powder all in a little cooking oil for starters. Add water, salt, monosodium glutamate (so who cares?), white pepper; chuck in some cinnamon, cloves, star anise and cardamom pods, and let it cook for 20 minutes. Then chuck in the tin of beef/mutton curry, and simmer another 10 to 15 minutes, topping up the water if it gets too dry. Blend a couple of dessert spoons of cornflour in some water, chuck that in, and stir until boiling again. By the time it's finished I have enough for my main daily meal for the best part of a week. I put it in the casserole dish in the fridge, together with a heap of cooked rice in the saucepan with the small handles. Each day take out enough of each for a meal, and heat rice and curry together in the saucepan - the rice is not so easy to reheat on its own, and I usually mix them as soon as they are on the plate anyway. The rice is cooked 1 part raw rice and 2 parts chicken stock.

My other main dietary ingredients are cream cracker biscuits taken with mackerel in tomato sauce, or tomatoes and cucumber. Instead of curry, I sometimes use the same vegetables and chicken stock to make a big pot of soup, but still with some rice in it. It's a cheap way to eat, and I can't afford the expensive ways at the moment.

The rain was pretty steady and consistent for the rest of the week, with the dirty laundry building up again. I don't like drying my laundry inside the house, because it nearly always ends up smelling a bit stale. Thursday saw the completion of *Bridges* 14, and I managed a quick dash to the shop during a short break in the rain. Then I stayed up all night writing *Bridges*

15, while it was flowing. By 11am Friday that was finished, and I had started writing 'Diana's Anguish', which had me in tears for a couple of hours.

I had just about dropped off to sleep in the afternoon, when Mohan the Rosella drink man knocked on the door. He cycles around the neighbourhood selling the new hibiscus extract cordial high in vitamin C. The manufacturers have given him the rights to sell to Singapore, but he has no contacts or organisation. We went to his house in town, which was an eye-opener for me. It is a big sprawling bungalow on about three quarters of an acre not far from the town centre - and I befriended him because I felt sorry for him! Apparently his father was an important man in the area, but spent his money on secret vices or something before his death. Mohan ended up with a big house and no money.

I used his phone to call Franky in Johor Bahru. Being Franky, he wants all sorts of things before he will act. Mohan was quite despondent after the phone conversation. So I explained to him that in order for Franky to help him, he would have to try and find a way to help Franky.
After an hour of talking to him and probing, I discovered that one of his father's old friends is a big man in Kelantan SADC. They are seeking about 200 workers for government plantations. Franky has 300 workers sitting in Indonesia, waiting for work in Malaysia – he says. I told Mohan to find out more about it, and get back to me with the information. If he gets Franky's foot in the door there, Franky will pay him good 'coffee money' - and try

to help with Rosella sales to Singapore and Indonesia.

It was after dark when I got home, and I was more than ready for an early night. But I felt an urge to get on with "Diana's Anguish'. Before I had got very far I was asleep at the computer.

CHAPTER 9

On Saturday I decided I should give the computer a rest, as my eyes were becoming sore and puffy. So I got on with wiring the model railway in the back room. By evening the trains were running, complete with weight/inertia simulation. I had a problem with the controller, the lead for which is nowhere near long enough to reach the closest wall socket. I have 2 extension leads, one of which powers the computer, printer and fan, while the fridge and washing machine share the other. Being unable to afford another one, I had to find an alternative method.

In amongst my 'junk' I have an old Australian extension lead and an extra adaptor plug. I put the adaptor in the outlet, and the lead into the adaptor. Then I cut off the Australian female end, stripped the wires, dismantled the British plug on the controller, spliced both sets of wires together, and reassembled the plug. It works - I just hope no electrical inspector comes along.

Sunday was the last day of what for me has been a most forgettable year. On Monday I started *Bridges* 16, but made little headway. Tuesday dawned bright and *sunny*. Everything else had to give way to the laundry, concentrating on the bed sheets, pillow slips, and towels for most of the day, followed by the most important clothing. In the evening I had another go at 16 - until 5.30 in the morning. By which time I had 20 pages to show for my sleepless night. Then I scrapped the lot, because it just wasn't right!

The stars were shining brightly, and I went outside to look

at them for a while. It's a long time since I've seen them so clearly in the northern hemisphere, having spent the bulk of the past 30 years in the southern. Most of my time north of the equator has been spent in cities, and most Asian cities are still very polluted. On the occasions when I have worked in the country I've usually been too busy to go outside and look at the stars.

By 3am it was *cold* - colder than I have ever experienced in this part of the world at sea level. I watched Rusdi and Ismail buying bed quilts at Tumpat, and others on the bus from Thailand similarly equipped, and thought they were all mad. Nobody told me it could get this chilly in the clear periods between Monsoon downpours. And here am I with nothing but sheets for my bed. I had 4 beautiful fleecy blankets while I was in Mt.Hagen in Papua New Guinea, where you know it's cold at night. But I gave them to my housegirl as a going away present, because I *knew* I wouldn't need them in Malaysia! I was sitting at the computer wearing a sarong over trousers, plus 2 shirts and a sweater. My sweaters I had also given away in PNG, but fortunately one of my waitresses in JB came from Kelantan, and lived in my house with some of the other workers. She was small, but wore outsize T shirts. When she disappeared, she left behind a sweater among a heap of other clothes, and it fits me. I've been asking Adam if he knows where to contact her, so I can give them back. When I asked Zainal in JB he said throw them in the garbage, but I didn't think that would be very nice; so I packed them up and brought them along - thank goodness.

According to Adam, the Monsoon here usually comes in 3 stages of about 3 weeks each, with 2 breaks of a week or more. That means when the rain starts again it will be for the final time. In the morning the sun was shining once more, so I washed everything else I had not yet washed yesterday - including the swimming togs I haven't worn for years.

Thursday was still sunny, so I went into town for Pasar Minggu (weekly market) and haggled for my fresh vegetables. I have a great time doing this, particularly with one toothless old lady who is a real character. We exchange insults and flattery in about equal proportions. When the bargaining is finished and the purchases made, we then have a chat, mostly about me and my family. I find most locals very curious to know why the hell I'm here at all! On the bus from the Thai border to Kota Bharu there is sometimes a European or two. The train from Pasir Mas to Johor Bahru contained at least one. But on the Pasir Puteh bus there ain't never no Orang Puteh exceptin' this old one!

Which somehow or other reminds me of the John Wayne toilet paper - it's rough and it's tough, and it don't take no crap off nobody. Or the new Russian jet airliner which had a distressing habit of shedding its wings. Until an Army colonel suggested they drill a line of perforations along the wing/body joint. 'You know how the Army toilet paper never tears at the perforations......'

The Indian boil-sucker joke? Never mind, it's in very bad taste.

I was in an Indonesian jail once - being held for no crime,

which is quite common in Indonesia - when there was a commotion outside. I suggested to one of my companions that it might be the arrival of the RAF low level penetration raid with our cold fish and chips and photographs of the Queen. He thought it was more likely Ross Perot with a busload of thousand dollar bills.

On another occasion, the Chief Prosecutor was using the guards' toilet, and a stream of moans and groans was issuing from behind the door. There were many suggestions as to what was going on, until somebody suggested that he had just discovered his bribery cheque from P.T. Surya Sakti had bounced. During my defence speech at the 'trial' I several times referred to 'Police Thief Alexander' and none of the judges corrected me.

On Friday the Monsoon came back, and I finally completed *Bridges* 16. My diary tells me that the Agent in Edinburgh, a Mr.McAra, should have received Diary 6-27(!) and *Bridges* 11 & 12 by now. I do hope he likes what he reads and acts as my Agent. If not, I'll just have to start all over again around the 30th or so - by which time it will be 9 weeks since I sent him the first lot. I like to observe the niceties with people, but if there is not even a postcard from him by then, I'll have to try somebody else. One of the nicer niceties is being able to eat on a regular basis! For all I know he might have given up the business since my 'Writer's Handbook' was published.

My large weed patch is fast becoming the local cattle pasture. I now have 2 bulls and 2 cows grazing as I look out of the (glassless) window. I spent Sunday and Monday outlining *Bridges* 17 to 20. On Tuesday I started the final draft of 17, and continued 'Diana's Anguish', which is a few years ahead, and very sad. That kept the hanky damp for half the day. The rest of the week was spent writing, editing and printing 17 to 20. Episode 21 was already in the computer. When the mood/idea/concept grabs me I sometimes write an episode from the future and fit it in as the story reaches it. As a result of this habit I started 22, and realized on page 5 that it's not 22 at all. It comes after the one in the computer marked 40, which I had just finished editing - and is 3 years down the line. Not quite as bad as 'Diana's Anguish' which is about 7 years and 5 pregnancies away!

On Monday 15th I had begun to worry about the rent from my JB house (empty wallet), due on the 11th, and late again, as usual. Kelantan will probably decide to enter the 21st century around 2010. Every month there are newspaper articles about sophisticated computerisation of some Government department or other. Everything is becoming quicker and more efficient all the time. But if you care to really look closely, you'll probably find it now takes most government departments longer to do things than it did 40 years ago. And for as long as officials can earn 'coffee money' by 'speeding up' one of their processes, nothing will ever be done quickly as a matter of course, no matter how many computers they have.

I went to see Adam, whom I haven't seen for a couple of weeks. He has been worrying busily over the impending birth of his new child. A baby boy arrived 3 days ago, mother and son doing well, and he is now back on deck. I told him about Mohan's father's friend's possible access to 200 jobs, on which Mohan has not yet got back to me. Adam promptly produced a letter he has just received from a large private plantation company seeking contract labour. The letter contained all relevant rates, conditions etc.

I put the letter in an envelope, together with a covering letter of my own, and gave it back to Adam. In the covering letter I suggested Franky might like to visit me after I return from renewing my visa in Thailand around the 27th. Since none of us has much money, a local operation would be much more suitable than trying to supply labour by remote control to the dam job in Sarawak. Though currently penniless, I do own a Malaysian Limited company, with paid up capital of nearly RM20,000 and no debts except to myself and the Company Secretary.

I was very careful to salvage it intact from the restaurant debacle for possible future use. If we secure labour supply contracts - or any other substantial business - we can carry them out under the company umbrella, with Adam and Franky as my fellow directors. On Thursday Adam came up with another proposition. A friend of his owns 6 chalets on Perhentian Island (Pulau Perhentian), a popular tourist destination out in the South China Sea. It is clearly visible from the beach house I am trying to secure. The friend wants to lease the chalets to someone on a cheap monthly rental. I told Adam

6 chalets are not really a viable proposition on their own. But we can go and look at them when I return from Thailand - by which time the Monsoon should be well and truly over. Resort facilities on Perhentian operate for 9 months of the year, closing down for 3 months over the Monsoon.

I did a quick search of my papers and produced my own design for a chalet resort. I designed this on the computer using Harvard Graphics - not an easy task. A CAD programme would have made things much easier. But when I borrowed the disks for such a programme, my computer sounded alarm bells and told me to take the first disk out, close down and re-boot - they were pirate disks. When Adam saw the contents of the folder he nearly fell off his chair.

It is a complete design, using a standard twin chalet layout as the basis for everything on the site. This can be erected in multiple, and adapted for use as restaurant/entertainment area, staff quarters, manager's house/office etc, all of which are covered by separate detailed floor designs. I have specified materials, done separate stump and floor bearers detail drawings and so forth. Plus a detailed estimate of construction costs; and operating costs on a 50% occupancy basis, including debt service - the lot in other words.

I originally designed the whole thing in 1993 for a proposed chalet resort near Mersing. It fell through because the land the owner put up as security was already mortgaged - that's Malaysia! At the time I also designed an alternative hotel for the site, with emphasis on natural light and solar energy. The

118

chalet design is maximum density, as there was only 3 acres available. Twice that area would be much better, allowing for extra facilities and/or future expansion.

When he had looked at my chalet resort design, Adam was as excited as a kid with a new toy. There is a 5 acre beachfront block for sale near Ismail's father's place for RM130,000 which is ideal. I mentioned the unspoiled beach there in a previous entry, when I visited Ismail's father. I held up my near-empty wallet for Adam's inspection, and he waved it away. He wants to photocopy everything and take it to his bank manager. As he says, we have a company, a design and a site - all we lack is the finance! I wished him luck. He might have some sort of reaction by the time I come back from Thailand. I have to stay out for 4 days this time - next time is a week minimum. Right now I'm not sure how I can afford a week, but I have 2 months in which to find a way. Maybe *somebody* will buy some of my scribblings by then. Though I understand from 'The Writer's Handbook' that publishers are not renowned for their fast draw, chequebook-wise.

I tried to explain to Adam that it might be possible to work my design in conjunction with the existing 6 chalets on Perhentian. Provided the lease is reasonable, there is enough land available etc. The way I have designed it allows for construction and operation in stages, as everything is a multiple of the same basic twin chalet design. But he was already up there in the clouds, out of reach.

I decided I might as well go to Thailand tomorrow,

instead of waiting until the last day of my visa on Monday. You never know, things might start happening in another week or so. I very much doubt it, but if they do, I won't be the one found unprepared. Adam found a buyer for his JB house in July, and the money still has not been settled. Adam's lawyer, the bank, and the buyer's lawyer have all contributed to the delay, by making mistakes and having to start all over again. But more important is the fact it's nearly 2 months since I had a beer!

The little kampong house is driving me slowly insane, or maybe I started out that way. I have no radio, cassette player or television, and sit talking to the computer and the animals from time to time. What I do have is a television set which took 8 months to arrive from Papua New Guinea, then fizzled out ten minutes after I plugged it in. Probably a spider's web shorted the whatsit gizzmo, know what I mean? Adam says he will get a friend of a friend to check it out while I'm gone, and if not too serious, fix it for a non-White-man price.

I caught the 10.15am No.3 bus on Thursday, and crossed the bridge to Thailand at 12.05 - my quickest trip yet. There was barely time for me to jump from one bus to the other at Kota Bharu bus station, as the No.29 was leaving as my No.3 arrived. But I managed to catch it in a traffic jam. Under the old system I would have missed it. Now, instead of entering at one end, and exiting at the other, on both sides of the building, they circle the building and leave by the way they came in. For some reason the other street outside the bus station has been closed. Maybe the buses were squishing more than their quota of pedestrians.

It never ceases to intrigue me how we human beings can distort our vision for the sake of personal convenience. If Malaysia had been involved in a war last year, and lost nearly 6,000 soldiers killed in combat, it would have been viewed as a national calamity. But to lose the same number of citizens killed on the roads is a case of shrug and get on with your own life. And it's just as true in most other countries of the world also. If there is a train crash in which 2 people are killed, it is headline news, regardless of the fact it may be the first train crash for months, and on the same day 15 or 20 people were killed by motor vehicles.

If the same rigid safety rules were applied to the roads as are applied to railways and aircraft, most people in the world would not be allowed to drive. Especially if the road users had to *pay* for the strict enforcement of those rules, as the railways and airlines are obliged to do. Then the roads *would* be a great deal safer. But just try winning an election on that platform! In the kampong here, there are dozens of children as young as 9 or 10 driving motorbikes around the roads and out to the highway. I have 2 policemen living next door to me, and neither of them has ever stopped any of those kids.

Twice I have refused to drive Adam's car until his young son is properly seated. He has the habit of standing between the front seats, completely unrestrained; with his parents - who should be seeing to his safety - encouraging him. I have explained my reasons to Adam, but he just thinks I'm being awkward. It's a sad world when a friend has to make himself unpopular in order to safeguard someone else's child. But I will *not* be the one driving the car when there is an emergency brake application, and that child smears himself over the windscreen, as a result of an 'accident.'

At Sungai Golok I settled into the hotel, and carefully counted my money. I am fed up with the austerity of the past four and a half months, and decided I would withdraw 300Baht (RM30) from my Bangkok Bank account. Provided the remaining balance of 300 is sufficient to keep the account open. This will allow me a bottle of beer on each of 3 evenings, plus a mild fling at the Andaman Cafe on either Friday or Saturday.

Having settled into my room at the Nam Thai Hotel No.2, I did some writing before venturing out in the evening to have a beer next door. Unfortunately there was a group of inebriated Indians gathered at 'my' pavement table, so I bought a packet of Krong Thip cigarettes and kept moving.

At the open air Chinese restaurant on the far side of the Marina Hotel I ordered fried rice, having eaten nothing all day. It went down well, accompanied by a large Carlsberg and Sprite for the Anderson shandy. It took me a few moments to recognise my usual Chinese waitress, who was dressed in jeans and lightweight sweater, with her long hair let down. The combination was much more attractive than before, and I gave her the thumbs up and a smile, which pleased her no end.

On Friday I went to the bank, and ascertained that 300baht was sufficient to maintain the account. With an extra

300baht in my wallet I made plans to spend the evening at the Andaman Cafe, whiling away the day with pad and pencil. Penny-pinching austerity is all very well, but one has to have fun some time.

I entered the Andaman at 8.30pm, glancing at the wall clock as I sat down. It was actually only 7.30 - I had forgotten once more the one hour difference when crossing the border. Consequently I was the one and only customer, and the girls gathered round for a chat. I had been looking forward to a chat with Lisa, but she is no longer the regular singer. In fact there is no longer a regular singer at all, management having decided to use the constant supply of amateurs every night, instead of on specific nights only.

Meanwhile the girls and I chatted away, mostly in sign language. Except for the ethnic Indian amazon selling titbits, who spoke quite good Malay. She worked away constantly at me to buy something, and I kept resisting, telling her I already ate thankyou. In the end she found a way through my defences by suggesting I buy one small packet of sotong goreng, and another of preserved mango slices 'for the girls, especially my sister'. Her 'sister', who was sitting beside me at the time, looked about as Indian as I do. But I consented with a grin, saying "For her yes, she's skinny enough to need it. You are already big enough."

Another girl sat down on my right and asked if I would buy her a chicken meal for 150baht. I said no way Jose, for that much I can buy a chicken meal at my Malay stall every day for a week! Or 3 large bottles of Carlsberg. She settled for a glass of my beer, with a grin which said no harm trying. Beer finished, she called another girl to take her place, telling her 'no money-lah'. I looked at this substitute as she sat down.

Her name is Nas - I think that's how you would spell it in English - and she is slim and beautiful. She tried my shandy, then got the waitress to fetch some ice and lemon with which to decorate her glass. She then proceeded to drink it through a straw, with a delightfully candid smile.

For the next two and a half hours she was content to share my shandy and chat away, between short stints of singing. She'll never be a threat to Maria Carey, but her singing is a cut above most of the others. And she pulls it off better in her long white dress, slit up the left side. Most of the girls wear scimpy outfits which are 'barely' decent, but Nas has an elegantly slim figure just right for the floor-length sheath. She is also taller than most, and has captivated me completely. Most unusual, as my normal trend is towards small, cute and cuddly.

When I say Nas is beautiful I mean just that. And I should know, since I have been married to two of the most beautiful women in the world (*really*, not just my opinion), and suffered through the hell of half the world trying to steal them from me. If you are like me, and listen to Dr.Hook singing *'When you're in love with a beautiful woman'* you know that whoever wrote the lyrics did so from experience.

For several years in the 1970s I was General Manager of a Brisbane construction company, during which time my first marriage ended and the second began. One evening we had dinner at the Ridge Hotel in order for the Boss's wife to meet the new Mrs. Anderson socially. While Liz (new wife) was at the ladies' room, Mrs.Boss leaned across the table and confided in me

"My God Braid, when I first met Donna (my previous wife) I thought she was the most beautiful woman I ever set eyes on. Now I've met Liz, I'm not sure any more."

Goddammit, surely at 55 years of age I should have learned by now - I even gave Nas the ring off my finger, I must be crazy. Living alone for too long seems to have softened my head somewhat, but why settle for second best? I never do, as witness my current state of near destitution. Writing is what I *want* to do, even though Construction Project Management is what I'm good at. But Project Management done properly is a full-time occupation, allowing no time for writing - so I stuck my neck out and gave it up.

I even want to spend on Nas the money I don't have, which is a sure sign of the old lunacy. Maybe she won't be here in March, thereby saving me from myself. Or maybe I can make it before March? Adam, how did you go with the bank manager? On the other hand, there's no fool like an old fool? Why knock it, just drift with the tide for a few hours.

By 10pm at the Andaman Cafe my wallet was empty, and there were a few more customers in the place. Nevertheless it could hardly be called a hive of activity, and I would venture the opinion that the management may be in danger of going broke if they continue to rely on only the amateur singers. I had spun out the contents of the wallet for two and a half hours; quite an achievement, considering it was hardly bulging when I entered.

At one stage Nas was called to sit with a gentleman who looked as if he had stacks of money to burn. Less than ten minutes later she returned to sit with me - maybe she's as daft as I am. During her singing stints she kept looking straight at me and smiling. *Oh, isn't it SO romantic Braidikins* - Casablanca removed to Thailand! When I got up to leave she accompanied me to the door, with a sad expression on her face. She seemed quite determined to see me again, despite my frequent protestations of 'no money'. I even received a peck at the door - it could hardly be called a kiss, as I was completely unprepared - to the accompaniment of applause from within. Either she is serious, or she is a better actress than singer.

Most of Saturday was spent recovering from Friday evening, following a long dream-filled night cuddling the spare pillow. We all have our fantasies more or less. Reality in the shape of my wallet brought the ground back under my feet. I had deliberately left 250bht at the hotel before going out, knowing my penchant for spending whatever I have on me when I'm having a good time. There will definitely be no more Andaman Cafe between now and Monday.

I went for a walk at 3pm while the cleaning lady did the room. Found myself accidentally walking past the Andaman Cafe - 3km away - twice! Then I took a wrong turning somewhere and hadn't a clue where I was. I have only been to

126

the Andaman before at night on the back of a motorbike taxi. Having wandered through a few strange streets, I spotted the microwave relay tower between a couple of buildings. That and the position of the sun gave me my bearings and I proceeded to wend my way through lots of narrow streets. Twenty minutes later I emerged straight opposite the hotel, from a new direction - not bad navigation. Mind you I was once a Navigating Cadet in the Merchant Navy, and an Artillery surveyor in the Army, so I ought to be able to find my way around.

I should have written down the street name and number of the Andaman while I was there. When I asked the hotel towkay to look it up for me in the phone book, it was not entered. I'll just have to walk there again tomorrow - drat it, what a shame. I want to write a letter to Nas telling her I will be back from 16th to 24th March at the Nam Thai, in case her stint doesn't last long.

On Saturday evening I decided the finances could stand one bottle of beer and a Sprite next door, after secreting bus fares to Pasir Puteh in the holdall. An Indian acquaintance from one of my previous visits was drinking inside, and probably thought me rude taking my bottle outside. But I can only afford one, and don't want to get in a 'school'. If I explained that to him, he would probably insist on buying me a couple of drinks, and I dislike scrounging off anyone.

I no longer feel obliged to drink all of my beer next door, as I am now charged the standard rate - the lady owner has decided I don't fancy her after all! There was a little

127

entertainment when the madame from the red light place took her dog for a ride on the motorbike. The dog didn't really want to sit up front with its paws on the handlebars. After three false starts during which the dog would not co-operate, they finally took off down the street - with three other dogs barking in hot pursuit.

The hotel towkay sat down for a chat, and was asking what Papua New Guinea people look like. I was in the middle of trying to describe them when I remembered I had a photograph of a PNG woman with my wife. I nipped upstairs to fetch the small album from my briefcase to show him. Having checked out the PNG lady, he then went through the rest of the album, with the usual comments on how small and beautiful my wife is. I know, I know, but the fact is she was lured to America three years ago by an American naval officer. I told her then that if she went, our marriage was over. She insisted 'only friends' but I knew better from the start, which was why I left the flat in Singapore and leased my house in Johor Baru.

But I am still in love with her, which is why I put the money in her CPF account, and got into the restaurant when she said she wanted to come back to me. Then I received the news that she was in a coma 'somewhere in America'. Maybe my stupid old-fashioned ideas on chivalry and such like, which will probably become extinct when I do. The story I received via family sources was that she and the boyfriend broke up a month before the stroke, and she wanted to come back to me, but was scared to try.

I set about doing all I could to locate her; something at which I am quite good. It once took me a single day to locate a friend from Britain on the opposite coast of Australia, armed only with name and occupation.

CHAPTER 10

I queried my wife's family on the strange fact that they knew she was in a coma, but did not know where. They said the ex-boyfriend rang from America with the news, but gave no details, and they didn't have his phone number. With what little information was available, I proceeded to place phone calls and send faxes far and wide. Singapore Foreign affairs, American Information Office, FBI, CIA, and anyone else I could think of.

The quaintest reaction I received to any of my queries was from the FBI. I rang the office in Washington DC asking for the fax number. The lady who answered informed me "I'm sorry sir, we don't give out fax numbers, you'll have to mail it."

Picture if you will, Special Agent Bloggs in Throngobia, having just uncovered the secrets of Throngobia's nuclear arsenal and their imminent intention of using it. He has a map of locations on him, but is being hotly pursued by Throngobian security personnel. He manages to disable the staff in one of their military offices which has a fax machine. All he can remember is the FBI phone number in Washington, so he rings them using the fax machine phone.

"I've got the detail plans of Throngobian nuclear missile sites, and they're planning a massive strike against the States tomorrow. Quick, give me your fax number, they'll be here any minute!"

"I'm sorry sir, we don't give out fax numbers, you'll have

to mail it." Beep.....beep.....beep.

The remaining replies mostly followed a common pattern, telling me too many hospitals in America, I would have to try narrowing it down; my reaction being that was what I thought *they* might help me with. The breakthrough came on the fourth day, when a letter arrived from a brother-in-law in Singapore, with the information that my wife's naval officer ex-boyfriend was last heard of in Florida. That narrowed things down considerably - a naval officer in Florida. I got out my half ton Rand McNally world atlas and started checking. Being an American publication it goes into considerable detail on the American scene - including all Army, Navy and Air Force bases, nicely marked in for the benefit of foreign spies.

I wrote down the names of every town within an hour's drive of every naval base in Florida - there are quite a few! Thus armed I paid a visit to the US Embassy in Singapore, and looked up hospitals and fax numbers in the listed towns. The Embassy has a very well stocked library, and the staff are most helpful.

By day 6 I had her located in a hospital in Port Charlotte, on the west coast of Florida, about 70 miles south of Tampa. Next thing was for our daughter to take leave from university in Australia and fly out there for a detailed report. What I received was not much more use than teeth are to a chook. The doctors have no idea whether she will ever recover from the stroke. If she does, they don't know how many of her functions she will regain or lose permanently.

I loved that girl, and gave her everything I could. Which according to her family was a large part of the problem. They reckon I spoiled Liz too much, and should have beaten her a few times. How can a grown man of 80kg strike a woman who goes on a diet when she exceeds 34kg? Mind you she has hit me often enough, but her attacks mostly just bounce off. One time in Brisbane she was having a go, while I read the Financial Review in the lounge. I took the paper through to the bedroom to escape, but she followed with tongue still wagging. Back in train to the lounge, where the Financial Review caught fire from her cigarette lighter, and was hastily doused in the kitchen sink. Return to bedroom, this time with the door locked and my back to it. Liz then kicks a hole in the door with one of her dinky little high heels, damned near spearing my back in the process.

That's enough, so I pick her up under my right arm, open the front door, place her outside and lock it - it's already dark outside. She rants and raves outside the door for ten minutes before circling the house and threatening to smash the laundry window. I tell her go ahead, but the repairs will come out of her next allowance along with the bedroom door if she doesn't behave. Finally she brings her main armament to bear and begins crying. Door open, friends again.

The moment I saw Liz coming down the stairs of my friend's uncle's house in Singapore, on 15th January 1975, I decided she was going to be my wife. I got the feeling I had known her for years, which was explained 10 years later. During my last year at school I began having a short dream, which was repeated on and off throughout the balance of my teens and twenties, before fading. It was almost like a photograph, so brief was it. There was this beautiful small woman sitting on a beach fringed with palm trees, while a young girl played beside her. They were both dressed in dark blue swimsuits trimmed with white.

One day in 1985 Liz, younger daughter Grace and I went to the beach at our favourite little sandy cove in Perak. A beautiful place off the back road to the rear gate of Lumut Naval Base. All of the tourist buses passed the turnoff on their way to the ferry for Pangkor Island and the Pan Pacific Resort, without ever suspecting they had missed such an enchanting retreat. As I came out of the water, the hair stood up on the nape of my neck. There ahead of me was the picture from that old dream. A dream which I first experienced the year Liz was born. Try explaining that one, I daren't.

On Sunday morning I set off to determine the address of the Andaman Cafe. Armed with notebook and pencil - which I carry everywhere nowadays - I walked up the street parallel to the one on which the night spot is located. Being broke as usual, I didn't really want to be spotted by anyone at the Andaman.

It is situated on an intersection, so I wanted to get both street names. This was not as easy as I'd supposed. Having spotted it on the cross street I looked for the street name, but there was none. I circled round to the far end of the cross street, and still no name. Then I checked the intermediate intersections, without luck. Next I made my way up to the top end of the main street on which the Andaman is located. Here I found a street name post, from which the name plate had been removed by vandals.

Finally I walked all the way down the main street, which is more than a kilometre long, checking every intersection. At the very bottom end of the street I found a street sign 'Vongvithee'. That would just have to do, and I hoped the letter would arrive at the proper destination. If not, I'm off the hook!

Back at the hotel I spent the rest of the afternoon and evening writing, and recalling once more some of the better times with Liz. She had a personality which could literally charm the birds from the trees. We were at the Buddhist temple in Happy Valley on Oahu one day. The specialty of the head monk is to call the wild sparrows from the trees and rooftop onto his outstretched hand, while the spectators stand back. Occasionally he will select someone to stand beside him and hold their hand for a bird to alight on. Sometimes it works, sometimes not.

As soon as he saw Liz he got all excited, saying she had 'the magic'. He called her over beside him, and straight away a couple of sparrows came down and settled on her hand, while the monk was not even touching her. A Japanese lady wanted him to do the same for her, but he said very sorry, it could only work for someone who had 'the magic'.

I used to get butterflies and dragonflies to perch on my upstretched finger in a swamp in Perak. But that was different -

134

they were after the salt in the sweat I had wiped off my forehead. It was in that swamp that I regularly saw the biggest butterflies I have ever seen anywhere - and I've seen quite a few in my travels. They were huge yellow creatures which usually flew in a formation of 3 to 5. They would beat their wings for a couple of seconds before gliding, just like yellow birds. In fact, the first time I saw them in the distance I thought they were birds.

In that same swamp we had to call the National Parks department to transfer a herd of wild elephants, who kept knocking over my road setout pegs. The monkeys were very brave and cheeky also sometimes. On one occasion a family group ran across the road in front of me, and one of the younger ones climbed a small solitary sapling in its panic. When I went for a close look at it, the rest of the family screamed, and started pelting me with nuts and berries from the higher trees! In that same swamp I ran over the tail of a cobra once in my Suzuki 4WD. Just as well I had the window up, because he reared and struck beside my face, with a noise like a stone hitting the window. Later I witnessed a fight to the death between a cobra and a mongoose. It was more than twenty minutes before the mongoose emerged the winner. One of the worst pests were the giant centipedes, up to 9 inches long. I was bitten on the toe by one when I had my boots off. The foot was painful and swollen for days.

A couple of Chinese friends tried my butterfly method and failed, simply because they hadn't the patience to stay still long enough. While a sergeant in the Artillery many years ago, I caught some of the famous Ghurkas the same way. One dark night I set up my men in camouflaged microphone pits, with strict instructions about no noise, no smoking, no movement. After seven hours, it was the Ghurkas who lost patience, moved first, and were caught in the trap. I employ much the same tactics with the ladies nowadays, though there was a time when I was much more impulsive. For more than two and a half years now, I have been waiting and watching, in the knowledge that maybe the right one will come along some day. If not, better to continue living alone, than settle for what is available rather than what I really want. It's a policy which sometimes makes life difficult, but also has its rewards. I've never been much of a believer in casual sex, nor do I believe in settling for second best. But living with such beliefs can become a strain from time to time. As a result of them I have not slept with a woman for 3 years, which will probably qualify me for the Funny Farm quite soon - or maybe I've already passed the qualifying exam!

At 4 o'clock on Sunday afternoon, a careful check of the finances showed that I could eat today after all. I went to my Malay stall and made my needs known to the hefty girl, who is much nicer than her slimmer mate. For my RM2 I received a fried chicken leg (the whole leg, not just the drumstick), a large portion of glutinous rice, dry fried onions, a small bag of sweet cili sauce, 5 lettuce leaves, 7 sprigs of coriander, and a fat spring onion. I couldn't have eaten much more if I tried.

Sunday evening at the hotel was spent catching up on

136

my writing, and thinking about Nas so near and yet so far. It probably won't work out, but the thought of her can at least make my life more pleasant for a short while. Not that I intend giving up the pursuit, which is not my way. But there are such trivialities as no job, no money, no speak each other's language, live in different countries, different nationalities, cultures and religion. But what would life be without a few problems to resolve now and then? That is after all what I've been paid for most of my working life. Even most people who marry same nationality, language, religion and so forth, are still of different sexes. And sometimes that can be the *big* problem compared to all the rest. Mind you, I do believe that Nas and I are also of different sexes - I hope!

Some time soon I will have to buy some new clothes. All of my trousers are at least 7 years old, as are my longsleeved shirts. The only relatively new clothes I possess are underwear and a few casual shirts. In 1987 I knew a plantation manager who had physically expanded with prosperity, prior to which he had been about the same dimensions as myself. He asked me to make an offer for his outgrown wardrobe, comprising 10 pairs of tailored trousers, 16 shirts and 2 safari suits. I jokingly offered a hundred Ringgit, and he accepted! I'm still wearing some of them.

Quite recently I said goodbye to one long-wearing cowboy shirt I bought in Denver in 1982. An elderly American lady in Denver came up to me, after telling her husband "Don't worry dear, I'll ask this nice cowboy." Meaning me, dressed in my cowboy boots, jeans, rhinestone shirt, leather neck thong and stetson. You can imagine the expression on her face when I told her very sorry I'm also a stranger here - in my Scots accent. By late evening I was thinking about Liz once more - maybe I'm just a glutton for punishment. In Brisbane once, the driver of the Rocket bus from Jindalee to the city insisted on charging my thirty-year-old wife half fare, while accompanied by her ten-year-old daughter. He thought they were sisters! Half the town reckoned I was a dirty old cradle snatcher. Except those businessmen and wives who were invited to the Andersons' place for Friday evening dinner. There was a long queue for this honour, because she cooks like an angel as well - not fair is it?

We were founder members of the 'Whispers on Wednesday Club'. This was the best disco in Brisbane at the time, where I parked the Trans Am in the reserved space out front, and handed the keys to the doorman in tails. He loved that car - exactly the same as Burt Reynolds' in the movie 'Smokey and the Bandit'. No matter what time we decided to leave, the doorman would have the keys ready, and the car parked in the place of honour at the front entrance - forewarned by the bush telegraph.

The first two occasions on which we dined at the Coronation - best seafood and Italian restaurant in Brisbane - they didn't have our favourite Moselle. On the third visit we were served it without having to ask - they had laid some down just for us. Ah, those were the days. Monday, back to the little yellow kampong house in Pasir Puteh!

Meanwhile I can just about afford spring rolls for supper, from the little stall at the night market, run by the charming sisters. Five spring rolls, a bag of sweet cili sauce, and three lettuce leaves for RM2. The literal translation of the street sign name is *Cheap Food Street* - it's not wrong.

I always thought of myself as not superstitious, but I'm not so sure lately. In 1987 a Chinese businessman friend and I went to Ipoh on business in his BMW. He was quite worried about the forthcoming meeting, so we left Sitiawan very early. He wanted to consult the most famous fortune teller in Ipoh, who gives away most of his fees to the poor. This was my friend's habit prior to important business decisions.

I sat in a nearby coffee shop for a long time awaiting the outcome of the session. When it was over, he asked me to have my fortune told, insisting on paying as an added incentive. It was a most comprehensive session, which took well over an hour to conclude.

First of course was my birth date, which established that I am a Water Dragon, which comes round once every 96 years. Then there was a prolonged examination of both hands, followed by a hands-on inspection of my head. He started off by telling me a few things about my childhood which opened my eyes and got him my full attention. Some of the things he told me were unknown to any of my associates in Perak. Like the time I was dragged from the water half dead; some of the nasty things my stepmother did to me, and so on. From there he moved on to more recent times, some of which he could have

139

been told by my friend, at a pinch. Though I don't know how he could have communicated all the information in the time. Unless that was all he was doing instead of having his own fortune told - which is possible, but unlikely.

For the finale I was told all about my small beautiful wife with the magnetic personality. But she would become selfish, and in a few years time we would be separated for 2 or 3 years. Then she would suddenly come back into my life as a completely different person. My lasting memory of that session was one of the main reasons it took me so long to get around to leaving Liz. Little did I suspect then how ominous that last bit really was.

On Monday I caught the bus back to Pasir Puteh and Puasa. Today is the start of fasting month. During daylight hours Moslems are not supposed to eat, drink, smoke etc. In Pasir Puteh that means no eating out, no tea at the coffee shop - so who has money to eat out anyway? My stay in Golok cost me RM150, house rent RM100, ink cartridge and paper for the computer printer RM80, electricity bill RM40. I spent RM50 on provisions and tobacco before leaving for Golok, which leaves me with RM80 of the RM500 from the rent on my JB house.

I sat down and worked out how to survive the 3 weeks until the next rent payment is due. Three large packets of cream cracker biscuits, three large tins of sardines, three tins of beef curry, plus three packets of tobacco comes to RM42. That's one of each per week. Plus a heap of fresh vegetables from the market at the rate of RM10 per week, still leaves enough to post a couple of letters.

On Tuesday I went to the shop and bought everything except the vegetables. Then set off to market, where I spent two hours checking quality and prices, before ending up with potatoes, onions, carrots, sweet potatoes, egg plant, tomatoes and cucumber for my RM10. The tomatoes and cucumber eke out the cream crackers in conjunction with the sardines! The rest go into my big casserole pot, along with one tin of beef curry as base, to make enough curry to last at least four days. I still have plenty of rice left in the container, plus curry powder, cloves, cinnamon, ginger, garlic etc. I will survive, but on strict smoking ration.

I'm getting a bit peeved with Adam lately. For a man who owes me RM10,000 he doesn't seem to be taking the situation very seriously. He was supposed to pay the rent on my house, but 'no money-lah', so that has gone bye-bye. Every time I see him he hangs his head and says he is broke. But whenever I go to the shop, chances are one of his two kids is in there, clutching a ten or five ringgit note, wandering around trying to decide what rubbish to spend it on. He has a nice house, car, phone, television, stereo, ceiling fans (which he just put in), none of which things I have. It is now more than two months since he contributed anything to my living expenses. But there is very little I can do about it while I am broke.

If I can sell some of my writing I will have a little capital with which to do things. But there has been no acknowledgement from the Agent in Edinburgh. I previously contacted several publishers and agents in England, U.S., Australia and Singapore. I did this 'blind' on information gathered from the British Highcom library. All of them replied, mostly with encouraging comments. Since receiving *The Writer's Handbook* I have written to one publisher and one agent in Scotland, neither of whom has responded in any way, not even a postcard. I may use some of the next rental income to place a person-to-person call to the agent. If he is not interested in my writing, it might be better to contact some of the newspapers and periodicals direct. I can worry about an agent for my books later.

I am determined to earn an income from my writing, and I will not give up yet, if ever. Far too much time, effort and creativity has gone into it just to give up without a long hard fight. Adam thinks I'm crazy going on and on at it, with no money coming in. But that's the Malay way - anything too difficult, shrug and surrender. It is not my way, and never will be. There was a letter waiting for me from my Company Secretary, which added a little humour to the day. He previously asked me for the financial statements when I requested he sell the company, so I sent him the day-by-day income and expenditure of the restaurant, which I have in the computer. According to him this is not sufficient, he would like me to 'have the accounts written up in proper books, together with bank statements'. I have written telling him - again - that I have no discretionary funds available with which to 'have..'. If he cannot do anything with what he has - which is also all I have - then put the company to sleep.

He charges RM100 a month to tell me what to do with money I don't have! I pointed out to him that the company has never had a bank account. After the third failed attempt to get myself, the bank manager and my Malay co-director in the bank manager's office at the same time, I gave up. Everything came out of my own pocket, including wages, marketing, the lot. Therefore legally and technically the company has not yet commenced to trade, so forget the twaddle and just make a Nil Return at the end of the financial year. We shall see what he makes of that - it will probably take him another month.

The rest of Tuesday was spent cooking, cleaning and washing laundry - a housewife's work is never done! In the evening I sat down at the computer and started catching up on the *Diary* entries - everything in Golok is written in pencil, then transferred when I return. When I finally got round to checking the time, it was 6 o'clock in the morning.

When I came back from JB I went to Telekom and asked them to disconnect the phone line in my JB house. They said okay, but I must bring back the handset. For more than a month I have been asking Adam for the handset. Every time he says yes, got, but he hasn't given me the damned thing yet.

CHAPTER 11

Wednesday Thursday and Friday were rainy days, during which I got on with the *Bridges* serial. On Saturday I was checking Things to be Done in my diary, and was annoyed by the fact that the return of the handset to Telekom has been dragging on for so many weeks. So I went to Adams' house and asked him for it once more. It was originally sent from JB by Zainal - as I was on my way to JB! As usual Adam said yes, got, give tomorrow.

On Sunday I returned to his doorstep, and he said oh, he hadn't got it out yet. I told him I would wait until he did, because I was worn out by all the trips I had made, and was determined to take it back today, not 'tomorrow'. In Kelantan Sunday is a normal working day. If I did not return the handset, Telekom would deduct it from my refund - at an inflated price. After much shaking of the head and muttering, he finally gave me the handset, and I set off to town. I had been making excuses all week not to go to town and post Nas's letter - it's raining, can go tomorrow etc. In the end I decided either I post it today or apply to become a Malay. Besides which it's about time I stopped playing the Martyr to Love Lost. There were two more letters to post - one to my company secretary, and the other to the Green Card Registration in Los Angeles.

The lottery for 50,000 American Green Cards is being held soon. This entitles the bearer to live and work in the U.S. I thought I might as well put my name down. Who knows what the future holds? There are some nice houses going at bargain basement prices in the Mid West 'ghost towns' and I can write anywhere. If I do generate some income from writing, maybe I can do Liz some good. Either way I will play things by ear - my crystal ball broke long ago.

I received a shock at Telekom. Before going inside, I decided to ring my number in JB from the public phone box, using the remaining credit on my phonecard. Imagine my surprise when I discovered it was still connected! I made haste inside with the handset, and asked what was going on. At first they said they couldn't check it from here, I would have to go to JB! I soon disabused them of that comfortable notion, telling them that this Orang Puteh was well aware of the fact that Telekom is a National organisation, interconnected by computer. I pointed to the computer terminals behind the counter, and the 'smart' man passed me through to a lady in the hinterland.

Half an hour later the explanation was that they had been waiting for me to return the handset. This is of course nonsense, but they have to say something, and that puts the onus on me. I also asked for a computer printout of the latest bill while I was at it, with my heart in my mouth. It stayed there as I discovered that my tenants have used the line to the tune of RM312.60 between 8/12/95 and 14/1/96. The 2 weeks since then is not available. I asked the lady to please make sure it was disconnected this time, and she gave me every assurance.

Once outside I phoned my house number again. After the

sixth ring, the wife picked up the phone. I said who I was, and heard the intake of breath, before I informed her that her husband must pay the phone bill, along with the next rent, on time, or vacate the premises. God knows what I'll do if they vacate, since I can't afford to go there anyway.

After a forty-five minute wait at POS Malaysia, I got my stamps and posted the letters. That was more than enough Government for one day.

On Monday I went to the local phone box and rang my house in JB once more - this time it was disconnected, thank God. I was annoyed with myself for not having thought to ring and check a month ago. But when there is no money, these things somehow seem less important. I simply presumed they would disconnect it when asked to do so, as it is in their own interest to quit while they are ahead. Now I am informed that my refund cheque will be mailed to me in 6 *months*! No prizes for guessing what happens if *you* take 6 months to pay *them*.

On Sunday afternoon I spent some time watching a trained monkey which was cleverer than his owner imagined. On the patch of vacant land between my house and the rubber plantation there are some floodlights for what I presume was once a volleyball court. In the usual kampong manner, it was probably started with plenty of enthusiasm for something new. Though I would guess it is no more than five years old, it is derelict and overgrown.

The owner tied the monkey to one of the floodlight poles by means of a loop in its chain. This particular pole is stripped of

146

its lights and appurtenances - probably by someone who needed them for his garden. Having spent some time examining his problem, the monkey climbed to the top of the pole, slipped the chain loop over, descended, and disappeared into the rubber trees!

With Puasa here, and Hari Raya therefore just round the corner, the children are playing with fireworks everywhere. One eight-year-old let off a rocket outside my house. It kept low, and crashed into the wall of the house next door. The occupants are two policemen, neither of whom reacted, despite the fact it is against the law of Malaysia for that child to be setting off fireworks. No doubt there will be a committee of inquiry when the next kid loses a hand.

On Monday evening I tried ringing the Agent in Edinburgh with a new RM10 phonecard I bought. Having got the unobtainable tone 6 times in half an hour, I walked to Adam's house, and asked if I could try from there. He told me his phone has been cut off for non-payment of the December bill. I wasn't wrong when I said no prizes for guessing what happens when *you* don't pay *them*!

Adam told me the local phone couldn't be used for IDD, and he had a visitor in the house. But he would come to my house at 9.30pm and drive me to town so I could use the one outside Telekom. 9.30 came and went, followed by 10.30 and 11.30, no Adam.

On Tuesday afternoon I took a taxi to town, only to discover that the phone at Telekom is also non-IDD. The nearest IDD public phonebox is in Kota Bharu, sixty kilometres away. What really annoyed me was the thought of having spent RM10 on a phonecard, which would have been much better spent on food. But it settled things in my own mind. Niceties or not, if there is nothing from the Agent in Edinburgh by the time the next rent comes in from my JB house in mid-February (due 11th, but never on time) I will send the first 10 Diary entries to a British newspaper. And each fortnight thereafter I will send it to another newspaper, until I receive a response. By 14th February it will be exactly 11 weeks since I posted the first lot to the agent; more than long enough.

The rats are trying to take over my house, and the damned rat trap won't work. No matter how I adjust it, they keep eating the bait without tripping it, then coming back for more, thanks very much. I can put it down baited on the kitchen floor, return a few minutes later, and the bait is gone! They scurry around in the roof at night, keeping me awake, and are constantly knocking things over in the kitchen - gives me the creeps, since I *hate* them.

I can't find anywhere that will sell me rat poison, though Adam says he knows where he can get some for me. No doubt he will turn up with it the day after the rats cart the house off through the rubber plantation - with me in it.

A chitchat just fell from the ceiling onto my computer keyboard. Gave me such a fright I nearly changed places with him on the ceiling. He picked himself up, looked apologetically at me, and scampered off behind the C.P.U. These mildly comical-looking little creatures are actually quite aggressive, and their quarrels can become long and loud. I watched a pair of them on the wall the other day. The slightly smaller one caught a moth, much too large to swallow in one go. Every so often the moth would flutter, and the chitchat would jerk his head from side to side, banging the moth on the wall. Meanwhile the larger one started to stalk his mate, staying perfectly still when the first one looked around, then moving again when he returned his attention to the moth. As soon as the second one got too close, the first one darted swiftly down the wall, moth still in his mouth.

After ten minutes or so of unsuccessful stalking, the second one turned his attention to a shiny thumbtack on the wall instead. He outflanked it stealthily, before suddenly swooping. There was a clearly audible thump as his mouth struck the thumbtack, and he retreated, nursing swollen lips.

Since I had bought the phonecard anyway, I rang Franky in JB to find out what he was doing about the labour contract. He said he didn't receive the letter Adam said he would post for me the day I went to Thailand. Since Adam gave me the letter in the first place, and I merely added a covering note, this was okay. I went to Adam's house, where he said yes, he posted it a week ago. Back to the phonebox I went to call Franky once more. I told him if the letter isn't there by Friday, get on the bus and come here, or the contracts will be lost.

He hummed and hawed, asking if I could go to JB instead. I said what the hell for? The contract is in Kelantan, not

Johor. Then he said could we meet in K.L.? I repeated, the contracts are here not there - one for a private estate which wants a hundred plus contract workers, and the other to supply up to two hundred day workers for the Kelantan State Government. Franky is the one who keeps saying he has three hundred Indonesian workers 'sitting waiting' for work in Malaysia. It is not for the customers to go to him, he must come to them. Sometimes I wonder why I have so much hair left.

The house is getting more like a menagerie. I was just confronted by a two-foot goanna in the toilet. For a moment I thought he intended disputing possession. But when I moved towards him he climbed the wall - literally - and squeezed out through the large gap between top of wall and roof iron. If he had stuck around I could have offered him a deal - like, clear out the rats, and the roof space is yours, rent-free.

On Wednesday I caught one of the neighbour's kids with his hand inside the window of my back room, where the model railway is, and he ran off at a high rate of knots. I closed half the shutters, as a safety precaution. But to close all is not feasible, since the back part of the house has no ceiling, just bare roofing iron. Close the shutters while the sun is shining, and the place becomes unbearably hot.

The weather was unpleasant for the balance of the week. Squally showers interspersed with gusty winds under a leaden sky. And I thought the Monsoon was supposed to be over. Nevertheless I managed to fit in the daily walk I had been urging on myself, in order to retain some semblance of fitness.

On Tuesday I set off - with umbrella - to explore the one direction in which I have not yet ventured. The narrow bitumen road gradually petered out and became an even narrower gravel road, with houses dotted about less frequently. There were more open fields than plantation, until the gravel road also petered out at a dead end with 3 houses round it.

I was about to turn round when I noticed a couple of schoolkids cycling out of the rubber trees to the right. On inspection I found a footpath winding through the trees. It was just wide enough to walk on, but looked as if it was used regularly. You can usually tell by the number of dead leaves lying on the track - the busier it is, the fewer the leaves. A hundred yards in I came upon the biggest spider I've yet seen here. It had a huge web spun between trees eight feet apart, and the spider itself was ensconced in the centre of the web. The span of its legs was at least four inches, with the body about two inches long by half an inch wide. It was basically metallic black, with bright blue streaks and creamy yellow splotches on the head and body. I saw more of them further in, but none as big as the first.

The track wound back and forth, without a single straight stretch. The rubber trees were being actively tapped, though there was a considerable amount of secondary growth. Half a mile or so along the path I came to a plank bridge across a tiny stream. A motorbike appeared from the opposite direction, so I got off the path to let him pass - it was a her. Another half mile and the track emerged in the middle of a small kampong with a narrow bitumen road.

I thought the road might swing round and join the one I had previously explored in the opposite direction from my house. But once through the kampong it swung off in the wrong direction, away from home, so I turned round to retrace my steps.

Once home I needed to bathe, but had to settle for a 'cat's lick', as the water has been off since last night, and goodness knows when it will come on again. Luckily the header tank was nearly full when it went off, so if I'm careful it can last me 3 or 4 days. About ten minutes after I got back there was a severe rain squall which threatened to rip the iron sheets off the roof. My umbrella wouldn't have been much good to me in that.

On the far side of the newly discovered kampong there is a small oil palm plantation, which brought back memories of years ago in Perak. I had one experience there which a plantation manager later described as something straight out of Somerset Maugham. Cannon Su and myself had been invited for dinner at the manager's house on the plantation, 15 kilometres from town - of which 5 kilometres is within the plantation. 'Cannon' was a local junior banker, whose wedding I attended. My wedding gift to him was a miniature cannon which I made from brass on my Unimat lathe - it even fired ballbearings. The plantation was the largest in Perak, and the commissioning manager Harold Speldiwinde was born in Sri Lanka of Dutch/local parentage. He had a taste for all things European, and dinner was something I hadn't seen the likes of for a long time.

We feasted on smoked salmon, venison, Danish ham, various cheeses and a heap of other imported goodies, topped off with imported Tuborg beer. It was the latter which did the damage.

When we said goodbye after midnight, Cannon insisted on driving my car, as I had drunk too much beer. Not far outside the gates of the plantation it dawned on me that Cannon was drunker than I was. The car was weaving across the road, and he had his foot flat down. I was about to tell him to stop and let me take over, when a power pole loomed up in the headlights. He swerved, sideswiped the pole, and the car took off - over the main irrigation canal. I later measured things on the spot, and the car flew through the air with the greatest of ease for almost a hundred feet, diagonally across the canal, before hitting the water.

My window was open, so it didn't take long for us to sink, with my side of the car underneath. Cannon panicked, and a babble of gibberish was coming out of his mouth. I leaned over to switch off the ignition, then heard my voice saying quietly "Would you mind opening your door before I drown here?" Cannon was above me, as the car had settled almost on its side.
He was still babbling, so I shouted "Shut up and get ready to push the bloody door." I reached past him and groped around for his window winder above me. When I found it I said "Hold your breath" before turning the handle. The water rushed in, relieving the pressure on the door. I then had to operate the

door handle, and *push* him to get the door open. Once outside with our heads above water, he tried to walk off - in the wrong direction. I just managed to grab his collar and haul him back as his head went under. By this time people had appeared from the kampong nearby, some of them with torches. I suffered bruises and a broken finger - my arm was outside when we hit. Harold pulled the car out with one of his tractors at daybreak.

On Thursday morning one of my model railway locomotives, worth RM140, was missing. Before jumping to conclusions I searched high and low for it, though I knew it should be about 3 feet from the closed shutter on the right half of the window.

Having searched inside, I then went outside, on the slight chance that it might have miraculously jumped off the rails and flown out of the window, by means of Divine intervention. On the ground outside the window was a pallet from next door's junk pile, positioned to allow someone to step up and reach inside my window. Obviously this had been put there by the kids next door, undetered by being chased away yesterday. Now there was not a kid in sight, so I knocked on the door of the neighbour's house.

I have two neighbours, this one behind, and the policemen beside my house. In front is the vacant and overgrown former volleyball court, with the road on the other side. Being 'kampong style' there are no dividing fences, and everyone wanders uninvited through everyone else's yard. There was no answer to my knocking, and the school minibus which the neighbour drives was not there. I worked at the computer with the window open, so I could see when he came back.

It was mid afternoon before he returned. I told him what had happened, showed him the model railway layout, described the kid I had caught with his arm in the window, and finally pointed out the pallet. He expressed regret with his mouth, but the eyes said so what, steal from the house of the Orang Puteh.

I let the rest of the afternoon and early evening pass by, waiting for him to move his pallet. In the end I moved it myself, satisfied that he couldn't care less. I picked up the pallet - which was quite heavy - and started rotating with it. Once I had a spin going, in the style of throwing the hammer, I let it go at exactly the right moment. It flew through the air beautifully, crashed into one of his house stumps and broke.

There was not a flicker of movement from inside the house as I stomped back round mine. For there to have been no reaction to such a crash on his house, I presume he had been watching from concealment inside - message received.

The weekend was spent setting up provisional appointments with the State Government and the private estate requiring Indonesian workers. Then ringing Franky to try and get him into gear, which is not the easiest thing to achieve. I am sick and tired of hearing 'the out 900 number you have dialled is not active, or is out of coverage' at least every second time I call him. In order to make the call in the first place, I have to change my clothes and walk out to the public telephone on the highway.

Franky cannot come immediately, must wait for 'new company profile', 'director coming from Jakarta' and so on. Which probably means he can't afford the fare right now! When I have no money, I say I have no money. But when Malays - which includes a large percentage of Indonesians - are broke, they will say anything rather than admit it. This also applies to many other things - most Malays I know would rather not tell the truth when a suitable lie occurs. In most cases they would call it being 'polite' and\or considerate of feelings - theirs or others. I still call it lying.

On Sunday afternoon Mohan turned up with a long face. He said he doesn't want to talk to Franky any more or do any business with him. It turns out that they have been talking to each other and making arrangements for weeks. Now Mohan is fed up, because 'Franky keeps breaking his promise to me, doesn't call me when he says going to. I don't trust him. Why should I talk to him any more when I have not even met him.' I let him go on at some length before getting in my bit.

I told him Franky probably thinks the same way about Mohan, since they have not met. That this is the first time I have been informed about their conversations and arrangements. Since they both know and have met me, why the hell have they not kept me in the picture, and so on. It also occured to me while I was talking that Franky may be under a misconception. Since Adam's real Malay name and Mohan's differ only in one letter, and sound the same on the phone, Franky may think they are one and the same person, and there is only one potential contract for labour supply. Especially as he did not receive Adam's letter.

I suggested to Mohan that we go to his house and telephone Franky together to sort things out. Once in contact with Franky it was agreed that he should come to Kelantan after Hari Raya. I agreed to this with some reluctance - more delay - but it makes sense. I know from experience that it's not much good trying to get things done during Puasa (fasting month) because of the general lethargy this induces in the Malay community - which is lethargic enough in normal times by Western standards.

Hari Raya will be on about February 21st. It is decided by observations of the moon, and some obscure calculations, I know very little about the details. Meanwhile all Malay restaurants and coffee shops are closed during the day. Which around the kampong means everything is closed, since they are all Malay.

I was back home by late afternoon, and went for a walk before dusk, through the rubber plantation to my 'new' kampong. On the way I met a coconut picker at the small plank bridge. His trained monkey was bathing happily in the small pool under the bridge, obviously enjoying his swim in the cool clear water.

CHAPTER 12

On Monday evening I was rather later than usual setting out on my daily walk through the overgrown rubber plantation. On the return journey dusk had already fallen. It's funny how the jungle seems so much less friendly in the dark! Next time I'm a bit late setting out, I think I'll take my torch.

Where the track emerges from the rubber trees at the far end, there is a small house - more like a shack - where an elderly lady lives on her own. The first time I passed she asked me where I was going, and I said just for a walk. Where did I come from? The other side of the plantation! Since then I stop for a brief chat whenever she's at home when I pass.

There is a coffee shop in the new kampong - call it Kampong Aman - which I must try once Puasa is over. By coffee shop I mean a shack with a couple of plank tables and benches. If I go there and sit down often enough, sooner or later people will start talking to me. Knowing Malay kampong people, it will be sooner rather than later - they are a naturally inquisitive lot.

The second day I went walking there, a middle aged man fell into step with me for half a mile, asking all the usual questions. Where was I from, where did I live, what did I do. There were raised eyebrows when I told him I live in a small kampong house on the other side of the rubber plantation, writing books.

No doubt he has spread the news by now, via word of mouth as substitute for a kampong newspaper. He would be sought after for a few days by the inquisitive, seeking free information they themselves are too shy to get direct.

Right now the rent from my JB house is due, and the money well is dry once more. Those tenants of mine worry me, with their casual attitude to payment, and non-sanctioned use of my telephone line. They seem just as likely to disappear one day without saying anything - and leaving unpaid bills behind. I hope I'm wrong, but that appears to be the way they are. If they don't pay, I have no money with which to go to JB and sort things out. If Franky would act as my agent, I could do something. But Franky looks for problems where there aren't any, never mind coping with real ones. Like the old man on his death bed, who said he'd had many troubles in his life, most of which never happened.

There is a rubber plantation backing onto the policemen's house beside mine. The sound of a raucous bird call was coming from the closest trees. I moved slowly and quietly to where I could see up into the trees, and waited for something to move. Within minutes I spotted them - the noise was being made by a family of small grey animals. They hopped around the branches, and as I stayed still, they came closer and closer; until they were less than twenty feet from me, and almost at ground level. They looked like a cross between a grey squirrel and a small Australian possum. Bodies about six or seven inches long, with tail longer than the body. The tail is furry, but not bushy. It flicks constantly behind along the branch, and can be used for holding on, like a monkey's tail. I watched them for about fifteen minutes, as they chased each other along branches, seeming to play like children. The raucous call I had first heard was not their only sound. They also uttered a much higher pitched sqeak every now and again, with the raucous one seemingly reserved for confrontation.

They broke and ran when I moved, in order to have a closer look at a butterfly that had flown past. I followed the butterfly into the plantation, where it led me a merry dance before settling on the low branch of a rubber sapling which was starting to flower. This was the biggest butterfly I had seen for quite some time. The main overall colour was luminescent bottle green, with a fluorescent light green horseshoe shape on the back. It had distinctive clubbed tails extending from the rear of the wings. While I watched, a second smaller one of the same colour flew past, and the first one took off in pursuit.

Most of the butterflies stick to the edge of the plantation, where there are plenty of flowering weeds at the moment. They come in a variety of sizes and colours, from the tiny yellow ones to the larger black and green ones. Occasionally I see a few medium sized bright blue ones with red and white markings.

The newspaper had an article on 'Balik kampong', which is literally back to the village. This is traditional on the last week of puasa, when there is a mass exodus from the cities, back to the home town/village. The Transport department has announced that this year there will be 1,500 express buses per day leaving Kuala Lumpur from 15th to 18th February - that's next week.

This year, for the first time in ages, Hari Raya and Chinese New Year coincide, whereas they are normally a month or more apart. So there will be mayhem on the roads, with many deaths to mark the joyous occasion. The express buses normally make a habit of breaking the speed limits as a matter of course. During festive seasons they simply shatter them. I have seen buses on the highway outside here, passing at a speed I thought barely possible, with the throttle wide open, engine roaring.

The balance of the week was spent printing out *DIARY* entries 1-10 with covering letters to a couple of newspapers. I would like to think the *Sunday Post* would publish it, but having been ignored by only the Scots so far, maybe better try farther south.

Monday and Tuesday brought squally weather, with rain and gusty winds. Consequently I stayed home talking to the computer, missing out on my usual walk through the plantation.

Wednesday dawned bright and clear, so I spent most of the day wandering around. First I went in the other direction, not having been that way since discovering the new kampong. But my steps soon turned round, leading back past my house and off in the new direction. There were still things to find out.

The biggest surprise of the week - of the year even - was to find a new street light between my house and the main road. There is only one, but that's a heck of a lot better than none at all. At least now, if I go out at night, I can leave my outside light on, and be able to see where I am going. On the return home, the new street light will supply an aiming point for the first part of the kampong road, with my house light for the balance. It also means I will now be able to see the bikes/motorbikes coming at me in the dark with no lights - there is no footpath, so one has to walk on the narrow road. This can be quite dangerous at night.

I presume the new street light is the local authority's Hari Raya present to the kampong community. For whatever reason, this is one thankful kampong resident. Hari Raya is the traditional 'spring cleaning' time for Malays. This is when they buy new furniture, renovate old, build extensions, and anything else to do with rejuvenating the house.

I have started calling Ahmad's place across the road the Istana Ahmad. An Istana is a lesser residence of royalty - lesser when compared to the main palace that is. He has had three men helping him to build an extension to the house since before Christmas. The house has already been extended several times in the past. It started off similar to Adam's place. He added another house the same size on one end. Next came an extension behind. This latest one is off the front corner, extending forwards and sideways. Last time I spoke to him I said 'selamat petang Datuk', which raised a laugh. Datuk is a title bestowed by the Sultan on outstanding citizens. In theory that is, though we all know the most deserving rarely receive, since they have no ear at court. But that has been going on since long before the Egyptians even had pyramids.

The first brickwork on the new Ahmad extension was somewhat less than straight, which offended me when passing.

I therefore lent him my long spirit level and a spool of bricklayer's string line, so he and his helpers could cause less visual offence. Then of course I had to demonstrate how to use the damned things properly. It was two hours before I could get away. Adam already has my staple gun for renovating his furniture coverings. I just hope they remember where those things belong. Malays as a rule have a habit of keeping things which they 'borrow' - witness my RM10,000 which Adam is no closer to repaying than he was six months ago. But in all fairness this trait is by no means confined to Malays - I can think of more than a few Europeans who have failed to return items borrowed from me.

This week the large candles and lamps are coming out at night, in preparation for the annual influx of visitors from the cities to the kampongs. Like the old Christian Christmas, this is the time for families to gather in the home town or village. Lights similar to Christmas tree decorations are seen on houses, and oil lamps or large candles are placed on the walls of the compound - provided the compound has walls. Those who have none, sometimes put a table out front with the lamps on top.

The fireworks are also hotting up, and the locals seem to be competing to see who can make the loudest bang. It matters not what time of the night it is either. Many Malays who have no regular day job - which includes many kampong people - stay awake all night and sleep during the day. This cuts down the hunger pangs, since Puasa comprises fasting from roughly sunup to sundown. This makes it a bit tough on the ones who have to do heavy work during the day. Adam sometimes comes to my house, where nobody can see him smoking. Though I'm quite sure Mohammed didn't include cigarettes on the fasting list!

I distinctly remember one Puasa in Perak, when I had a member of the Perak Royal family as my partner in a business venture. Royalty are traditionally the guardians of the Moslem faith. We were sitting in the government guesthouse in Lumut just prior to the official finish of fasting for the day. He kept checking his watch - every town has its own time, to the minute. He told me to go ahead and order my food, while he waited for the official time to arrive. When it did arrive, I was half way through my dinner, at his invitation. But contrary to my usual habit, I didn't order a beer, in deference to his beliefs. Imagine my surprise when the first thing he ordered at the starting line was not food, but a beer - for himself. Moslems are not supposed to drink beer at any time, never mind Puasa! I had my own beer on the table in record time after that.

At that time the Perak royal family had shares in the Jockey Pub and the Pink Flamingo night club in Ipoh. The third in line to the throne also tried unsuccessfully to take over the nightlife of Sitiawan at one time. During this period some of the local nightclub and pub owners had a pretty lean time with the new District Officer breathing down their necks.

On Thursday Adam's wife returned from Johor Bahru. She went to my house in JB to see if she could bring back the rent, but there was nobody there, and it was all locked up. The rent is 4 days overdue. Adam has tried contacting their mobile phone without success, as I have no money left. Adam's wife gave me RM20 to tide me over, so I bought a packet of tobacco, tea, milk, a tin of mackerel, and cracker biscuits, which left me with RM5.

I have to post the first 10 Entries of this diary to a newspaper, but even that will cost at least RM12. Meanwhile I have no idea if my tenants are still occupying my house, or have done a bunk, having used my phone line to the tune of a month's rent. And with no contact on their mobile phone I have no way of finding out. I wish Adam's wife had thought to go round the back and look in the kitchen window to see if their furniture is still there. A few more days and I will be literally destitute.

With nothing else to do, I sat down at the computer to organize the later *Bridges* writing into proper serial episodes. I had the outline for a book, which I have now filled in. Episodes 1 to 25 are finished, with the basic (very basic) outline of many more episodes in chronological order. When I finished counting I found that the new ones will be roughly 75 to 97. Each episode is 3,600 words, so 24 or 25 make an average size book. I hope and pray somebody will buy it. There's some really good stuff there, though I say it myself.

By Saturday evening I had 75 and 76 chopped, changed, and edited, when Mohan came visiting. Franky called him and said he will be in Pasir Puteh the week starting on the 26th, which is after Hari Raya. If we get the labour contract/s Franky wants Mohan and I to supervise and 'look after' the workers. I said that's good, except I have no transport, and we won't get far on your pushbike! The look on his face said this hadn't even occurred to him, and I nearly burst out laughing. Then he said Franky would have to supply transport, to which I commented that would mean working for Franky. Right now I don't think Franky can afford his OWN transport, which is probably a large part of the reason he wants to give out the supervision contract. Anyway I have a better idea, which entails Franky giving the supervision contract to my company, in which Adam and Mohan become directors. Adam can always supply transport via his friends in Kemaman. We drive round in the current vehicle for sale, until it's sold, then collect another one. When Mohan left I walked to Adam's house to confirm this would be possible, and he said no problem, can do.

Here goes the penniless Castaway trying to do big business on an empty wallet and very soon empty stomach! The supervision contract on a couple of hundred workers is not to be sneezed at. It would keep all three of us with roofs over our heads and food in our stomachs very nicely thankyou. And unlike a one-off business deal, it would be ongoing, for as long as the customers are happy with the labour. Besides which it's always nice to work with someone else's money rather than your own - ask any banker.

On Sunday it rained, after a few sunny days. But it was ordinary rain, not the Monsoon type, thank goodness. By not long after midnight episodes 77 to 80 of the later *Bridges* were complete and tucked up in bed - followed immediately by myself.

Monday was very squally weather, with strong wind gusts, and intermittent showers. New *Bridges* 81 to 84 were completed and added to the file. I have decided to split the episodes into 4 files, with 25 episodes in each file - 75 etc are in *Bridges4*.man. When I finish tidying them up, all I have to do then is write the episodes in between - all 50 of them in *BRIDGES* 2 & 3! As soon as an episode is finished I add it to the file. Then I copy it to the same file on my backup disk on Drive D, AND onto a floppy disk - it's called belt and braces. When I bought the computer to make my writing easier and more secure, I had never touched a computer in my life. I shopped around in Singapore for the best buy, then packed it up and took it home. No computer course, no software manuals or disks - but I did have Direct Access. I set it all up, plugged everything in, and started talking to it. During the familiarization process I somehow managed to wipe my Spellcheck utility and a few other things. But I got the hang of it eventually.

Now when the computer complains about something I do, I frequently tell it what a dumb machine it is. If - sorry, that's when - I have some money coming in from my scribbling, I would like to invest in a new computer and hook into Internet. Then I can do research which I really need to do already - particularly on world events, dates, places in the '60s decade.

I thought of updating my present computer; but it would be better to buy a new one, and keep this one as the dedicated writing machine. To fix it up with multi media, extra memory, modems etc would cost more than half the price of a new one with everything installed. *and* I would still have all my eggs in one old basket. I already put an extra hard disk in, but I still have less than half the memory of the current budget priced multi media sets. If this one becomes the dedicated writing computer, I can wipe every unnecessary programme, and be left with all the memory and backup I will ever need for writing.

I stayed up all of Monday night sorting out *Bridges* 85 to 90. Sleep would have been quite difficult in any case, as the fireworks were reaching a crescendo. One more day to get through before Hari Raya finally arrives - or so I thought. Which reminded me that the shops would be closed for a few days, so I'd best invest my remaining RM5 in RM4 of vegetables plus taxi fares to market.

I was standing out on the highway before dawn, waiting for a taxi. Over a period of half an hour, at least a dozen passed me at over 100kph without even slowing down. In the other direction an almost continuous procession of express buses thundered by, not one of them within the speed limit. The highway was so busy I began to think maybe I had somehow wandered onto the wrong one nearer the national capital. Vehicles doing a mere 120kph were being overtaken by others doing 150 - sometimes forcing a vehicle coming the opposite way onto the road shoulder. Having watched this for half an hour, I cancelled my trip, and returned to the safety of my little kampong house - well clear of the highway. I might as well grab a couple of hours sleep. Just as I lay down, there was a knock on the door, and a call from without. It was Ahmad's second son, dressed in all his Moslem finery, come to invite me for Hari Raya breakfast at his house.

The penny dropped - today is Hari Raya, not tomorrow. Adam told me it was the 21st. Obviously he was mistaken, since today is the 20th. Then again, maybe he thought he was right when he told me, since the actual date is only announced at the last moment, via observation of the man in the moon. Just as well I couldn't get a taxi, or I would have wasted the taxi fare - the market will not be open today of all days.

I sat in the latest extension of Istana Ahmad eating breakfast, and greeting new arrivals - I was the first of a long procession. Ahmad was dressed in his long white robe, with white songkok atop his head, heaping blessings upon all and sundry. He seems to be doing remarkably well out of the bomoh (traditional medicine man) business.

Half an hour after my arrival the place was becoming crowded, so I thought it best to create a vacancy by departing. Having wished everyone 'selamat Hari Raya' I bowed my way out the door and off across the road to my own more humble abode. I was about to try for a sleep once more, when there was a screech of tortured metal from outside. One of the departing guests from across the road had been turning his car, and put a wheel in the drain at the (unguarded) end of the culvert. The car looked rather forlorn with the left rear cocked up in the air. A crowd soon gathered, but nobody seemed sure of what to do. Half a dozen started pushing from the front, which did no good at all.

Having watched for ten minutes, I thought I'd best lend a hand, or they would be at it all day. Some surplus materials from Ahmad's recent house extension were still stacked in a corner of the yard. I selected a 10ft length of 4" x 4" timber and lugged it across to the stranded car - it was quite heavy, being hardwood. With the bottom end fitted snugly under the right front wheel in the culvert, I then gave instructions to the gang of helpers, in my best Project Manager style.

Three men sat on the cocked up corner of the boot, with four more lined up along the front - with instructions to LIFT not push. They were to watch me and lift when I nodded my head. I told the driver to get in the car and put it in reverse. When I nodded my head he was to rev up and drop the clutch. I leaned back on my 'lever', nodded my head, and out she came first time.

The rent from JB has still not been received, and not much chance within the next week now, with Hari Raya AND Chinese New year jamming the nation's communications systems solid. Groups of kids started calling to wish me Selamat Hari Raya, and I felt bad having nothing to offer them. Until it occurred to me that a look at the model railway in operation might be better than a sweet to most of them. The next lot were invited in, and spent half an hour watching the trains shuttling back and forth. I placed some kitchen chairs for the smallest kids to stand on, and a good time was had by all. When I called a halt, they went off and told all their friends. The rest of the day was spent operating the layout for successive batches of kids - they must have put the word round the whole kampong, because until now I didn't realize there were so many kids in the entire neighbourhood. If I was making 50c per entry I would have collected enough to post *DIARY* 1-10 to more than one newspaper!

Wednesday was a repeat performance, with most of them back for a second look. My operating was getting pretty ragged, and more than once a train hit the end wall in the fiddle yard, because I couldn't see through a dozen little heads. There are normally five trains stacked in the fiddle yard, plus one each in the distillery sidings and station goods yard. It takes about half an hour to complete the whole sequence, with each train doing its short out and back trip. The locomotives on the passenger trains run round the loop to the opposite end of the train before returning. The goods trains shunt in the distillery and goods yards and depart with different wagons. Later they return for their original wagons.

CHAPTER 13

The words just wouldn't come at the computer, and I was flat broke, with an empty fridge. So I reminisced about Liz once more. She was so full of life before the coma, it's a double tragedy for her to end up this way. Once when we stayed at Ceasar's Palace in Las Vegas, she was mad because we were leaving the day before Tom Jones was due to perform. Cher was on, but she wanted Tom Jones - I think Cher's very talented myself. As consolation Liz made an appointment at the hotel hairdressing salon. She was there for five hours(!) before I received a call on the house phone to pick her up. When I saw her I nearly fell over - her hair was frizzed out all over the place. I said "My God Liz, there are negro women in this country who pay a fortune to get that *out* of their hair!" It didn't faze her one little bit.

In Puerto Vallarta Mexico (where we visited The Love Boat), we were sitting in the open-sided restaurant at the edge of the beach eating lunch. Liz asked the waiter for *hot* chili sauce and was unhappy with what he brought. "I want hot chili sauce, this isn't hot." The waiter raised his eyebrows, and returned with the sauce boat five minutes later, hanging around to watch the(he thought) explosive result. Liz tasted a big spoonful and said "That's no good, all you did was empty a bottle of Tabasco into it - I want real hot chili sauce." The waiter departed, shaking his head in disbelief.

The same sort of thing happened at a Thai restaurant in

Sydney, where I told the waitress "If my wife's chili seafood is too hot, that's my fault, if not hot enough, your fault, okay?" They couldn't resist a challenge like that. When the food arrived, it was followed by the cook, who wanted to witness the consumption. It was so hot he had been scared to test it himself. Liz ate the lot, with the comment not bad at all, the best she's had in Australia. Two years later I was in Sydney for a meeting with the Coal Board Tribunal, in the company of the President of the Combined Miners' Union. He wanted to eat Thai food, so I took him to the same place. The owner remembered the small beautiful woman who could eat the hottest chili, and sent out for takeaway containers, so I could take some special chili seafood back to Brisbane for her. They don't normally serve takeaways at all.

In Brisbane I won many magnums of champagne on Liz's ability to eat the hottest chilis. One earthmoving machinery parts dealer reckoned his sister in Cairns grew the hottest chilis in Australia, which *nobody* could eat raw. He went to the trouble of having her airfreight a tube of them to Brisbane. When they arrived he hotfooted it to my place, and hung around for the moment of his triumph. Liz chewed away, until they were all gone, as Paddy's eyebrows grew closer and closer to the sky. Then Liz asked

"When are the hot ones coming Paddy?" We shared the magnum.

This same Paddy and I had a few run-ins, as he supplied most of the wear parts for my bulldozers, and I liked to take my

173

time paying. Sometimes I would toss a coin in his office. If he called right, I would pay the bill up to date, if not, it went out to 90 days. One day when he lost, he passed the comment that it was no wonder I could afford the beautiful lined leather jacket I was wearing. I took it off there and then, and exchanged it for the work jacket he was wearing. That guaranteed the 90 days.

One day when I was in an unusual hurry at payment time, I signed all of the cheques presented by my secretary without checking them individually - not a normal habit of mine. Three days later, when I got round to entering the cheques in my private ledger, I almost had apoplexy. I had signed a cheque bringing Paddy right up to date. I promptly wrote him a letter, together with an order form for dozer grouser plates and a couple of idlers for a D9. The letter went something like

"Dear Paddy, I very much regret that, due to a most unfortunate oversight on my part, your bill has been paid up to date. In order to rectify this deplorable situation as quickly as possible, please find enclosed an order for supply of parts, for which I promise not to pay in less than 90 days."

He sent the letter to head office in Perth, with the comment 'see the crazy people I have to deal with here.' They framed it and hung it on the office wall - and I got my 90 days. In Papua New Guinea I had a problem with the seal coat applied by my subcontractor on the sports complex road diversion. The boss knew damned well he had to fix it, but for more than a week he was 'not available' every time I called. In the end I sent a fax addressed to Starship Shorncliffe, Seventh

Nebula, Outer Umpteenth Galaxy

Dear Astronaut Omi

NO TOUCHDOWN, NO MONEY

He was on site less than an hour later.

Back in the kampong, the kids were knocking on the door again. I got up to open the door and tell them to go away and stop bothering me. A little face with enormous eyes looked up at me "Uncle, boleh tengoh kreta api?" "Okay, but ten minutes only" said I with my most stern expression. The small face was followed in the door by about twelve more - I didn't count. Half an hour later I said goodbye and ushered them all out.

The railway layout is not the most entertaining for children, being a mere shuttle service - maybe I can improve on that.. I suppose to most people I must appear crazy, sitting here flat broke in my little kampong house. Instead of drawing down ten thousand Ringgit per month as a project manager, plus free house, car, electricity and housemaid. But anyone who knows me well enough can tell you I'm nothing if not really stubborn once I have my mind set on something. And right now it's set on earning a living from writing. It's not quite as daft as it may seem at first sight. I have no pension or superannuation, and in a few more years I will be considered 'too old' by most companies who employ my kind in the odd corners of the world. I can write anywhere anytime, for as long as my brain still functions. Besides which, it's something I've wanted to do for a long time.

Mind you, if my tenants don't pay the rent soon I will be in very dire straits. I would hate to have to go cap in hand to the

British High Commission for help. They prefer helping foreigners to helping their own. If you don't believe me, try reading my book *Tropical Trial* - if Maggie Thatcher ever lets it be printed.

IF they did anything at all for me, it would probably be to sue Adam's Agency for my RM10,000. I'm not quite ready for that to happen, though it may not be long before I'm left with no choice.

Whether any money could be squeezed from Adam right now is in any case a moot point. If I could raise the spare money to send this *Diary* to a few newspapers in Britain, I'm sure one would buy it. But I don't yet even have money to send it to one newspaper. Come to think of it, I *must* be crazy.

Cars are arriving and parking all round my house, in preparation for the big wedding procession. Adam's cousin is marrying my next door neighbour's sister. I was invited, but politely declined - I have no money to buy a present, and I'm certainly not going empty-handed. Any way, I've been to enough Moslem weddings already - and Chinese, and Indian et al. This one will go on for several days.

Today is the actual wedding ceremony, but during the next few days, the families of the bride and groom will hit the road in large squads, paying calls on their opposite numbers in the other family. I dare say I might be hungry enough to reluctantly accept an invitation to the final feast next door on Sunday!

I spent most of Friday, Saturday and Sunday morning sorting out the balance of *Bridges*. Meanwhile large numbers of cars kept coming and going next door. At one stage on Saturday I had a squad of overflow people on my front doorstep, making a hell of a din with their chatter. On Saturday Zainal turned up, which reminded me that I still have Aziza's clothing here. I thought I'd best check it out. She was one of the waitresses in my restaurant in JB - half of them lived in my house.

The clothing has been in a large cardboard box under the railway layout for months, and probably needs washing. That was an understatement! When I checked, the rats had been using the box/clothes as a nest, and it was full of rat droppings, nut shells, and bugs. I emptied everything out in the back yard, then sorted the clothing into two piles. One pile for washing, the other for those not worth salvaging.

I threw the spoiled lot - about a quarter of the total - in a plastic bag and dumped it in the dumpster out on the highway. Then on Sunday morning I washed all that remained. Meanwhile the big feast was on next door, and the neighbour called to invite me to eat. I said thanks very much, maybe later, not wanting to go on my own. Adam turned up later and said okay let's go. He came at the same time as a large 50-seat tour bus, which parked on the vacant lot and disgorged a full load. This was Adam's Bachok family connections come for the feast!

We sat down at a long table and were served rice on a plate, then help yourself to curry, vegetables etc. But first hold your right hand under the kettle of water before plunging it into the food - no cutlery. That's why the strict Moslems won't eat

177

with a convicted thief. The right hand is used for rummaging in the communal food bowl, while the left one is reserved for washing the brown stuff off your backside. Fundamentalist punishment for thieving is to cut off the right hand.

Adam's wife had the new baby boy with her, and couldn't go inside to eat with the other women - the sexes are strictly segregated at these functions. I hurried with my food, then went over to where she was sitting apart on her own. I told her to give me the baby, while she has some food. This raised quite a few eyebrows among the male gathering, but I dislike bigotry in whatever guise, so the hell with them.

For fifteen minutes I sat surrounded by men, feeding the baby his bottle. When he wanted to cry, I burped him, then went for a walk under the awning, rocking him and patting his back. He behaved perfectly, and Adam said later I was the only stranger so far who could handle him without a wailing session. But with eight of my own, I've had plenty of practice - including delivering one and suffering the labour pains for another. Funny how both of them were girls, never any problems with the boys.

After the feast it was time for the kids' big model railway exhibition. I turned round from the controls, and there was Aziza, whom I haven't seen for six months, and whose clothes I only today washed - I must be psychic.

I look out the window, and there goes another ten year old driving a motorbike - with passengers aged roughly seven and four. Adam turned up with a container of his mother's curry and a ten Ringgit note. I got changed, grabbed the large envelope containing the first 10 entries of this Diary, and headed for the post office. It cost me RM12 to post to a British newspaper, plus taxi fares, leaving me flat broke once more. But at least I have enough of Mum's curry to last me a few days. Thank God the Diary is on its way at last; now I can only pray they like it.

I'd like to get my hands on the Agent I put so much trust - and money - into. It wouldn't have broken him to send me a postcard, especially as I explained my position exactly in the covering letter - and said I would wait sufficiently long for a reply before contacting anyone else.

The house owner came on Sunday night, looking for the rent, and pleading poverty. While her husband sat in the large shiny new Honda car out on the road. I told her I have no money until or unless my tenants in JB pay me, and they are already two weeks late and uncontactable. In any case, until now I have had no dealings with the owner. Adam got the house and was supposed to pay the rent - which went by the board as soon as I moved in. But at least I know Adam has problems also, and is trying his lopsided best to help me. Whereas the owner is just a greedy liar - I should have offered to pay her in rats. Or pay him in rats, since I think he's the greedy one, getting his wife to do the dirty work.

Franky is supposed to come this week - we shall see. I once wrote (*Tropical Trial*) that British Embassies are so big, in order to house all of their excuses. Something similar could be said for most Malays - but don't get me wrong, I like most of them anyway. It's just that their dilly-dallying ways can get up the nose of someone like me, no matter how hard I try to adjust. When you have spent 30 years as a construction project manager - which by definition is go-go-go - it takes a lot of effort to learn dilly-dally.

On Tuesday the two-feet-tall gang were back to see the model railway. I told them come back tomorrow, the railway is closed for extensions. From 10am to 6pm I was very busy sawing and fitting some of the spare plywood I brought from JB to extend the layout right round the back room. That's the room with the bare corrugated iron roof - no ceiling or insulation - so I must have sweated half a gallon by the time I finished.

By 6pm the timberwork was complete, track laid and wired, and the first train circumnavigated the new extension loop. Unfortunately I had no champagne with which to celebrate, and settled for a cup of teh wangi ros - that's rose-scented tea. There is a long gradient on the new circuit, with the summit at Bukit Dapur (Kitchen Hill). The 0-6-0 goods engine labours up the gradient most realistically with a train of 25 coal wagons, then gains a bit of speed down the other side. The Class 25 diesel with 5 Gresley coaches also loses speed on the bank, but the slope is just enough to be realistic, not ridiculous. What IS ridiculous is this ex-project manager sitting broke in a Malaysian kampong house running a model railway for the local kids!

I tried several times to raise Franky via Adam's phone, without success. The lines are still jammed up from Hari Raya and Chinese New Year coming together. Adam has just

180

suggested that I should go to Kota Bharu with him and 'bark' for his friend's hotel/hostel. He says there are plenty of 'orang putehs' around at this time of the year, and I should talk some of them into staying at the right place. I'm game, but I want to see the hotel and check its rooms and prices, before I take anyone there. Adam said okay, we go and have a look next time I go to Thailand for my visa. I said why wait two or three weeks, if my tenants pay the rent at the weekend, we can go Monday. It will give me something else to write about.

I finally raised my tenants on their mobile phone. They are 'balik kampong', about half way between here and Kota Bharu. They have promised to come at the weekend and pay me up to date. One week after that and it will be time for the *next* month's rent. It may seem funny at a distance - in kilometres or time - but right now it's not funny having empty fridge and pockets.

Wednesday was gala day for the new railway extension. There was a procession of children most of the day, with plenty of satisfying oohs and aahs. I can now run one train round the continuous circuit on controller 1, while operating a shuttle service between the fiddle yard and the station on controller 2.

I time things so that the shuttle meets the main line train at the crossover outside the station, where they converge on each other from opposite directions, before passing with an inch to spare. This usually brings a few sharp intakes of breath. No doubt most of the little devils regret the fact that the trains just miss instead of crashing into each other! Any one of the seven trains can run either on the main circuit or the shuttle service, with a minimum of fuss and bother. Occasionally I do worry a little about my Heath Robinson wiring arrangements, with the Australian extension lead spliced into the British plug, from the Malaysian outlet - but only when I remember.

On Friday I set off on my usual walk to the new kampong, with my mind set on no longer retracing my steps. In the first plantation the stream beneath the plank bridge had dried up, leaving only a shallow stagnant pool. Less than two weeks ago a trained monkey was having a swim in there - now it wouldn't even reach his knees. Everything is drying out very quickly now the Monsoon is over. Most of the drains have new growth in them already, and it won't be long before even the pool under the plank bridge disappears.

Where the new kampong road veers left in the wrong direction, I decided to strike off through the rubber plantation to the right. Given decent navigation - and tracks of any sort - I was confident in my ability to find a new circular route back home. At first the track was well defined, but four hundred yards in, it too swung off in the wrong direction. I then followed the narrow rubber tapper's pathways, until they also became almost non-existent. But cattle or goats had been through, so I was able to continue in what I estimated to be the right direction - with deviations for impassable areas.

The rubber trees thinned out after a kilometre or so, and I was into an area of secondary jungle growth. But having come this far, I was not about to give up easily. I plodded on, weaving a path through the easiest going, collecting plenty of spiders' webs on the way. Until I came out on a more open area, where a couple of cattle were grazing. This looked like it was a wide shallow stream during the Monsoon, but now it was grass and mud.

There was a faint track on the other side, presumably used by the boy who looks after the cattle. Looking around to get my bearings I estimated this to be a continuation of the stream under my plank bridge, about two kilometres downstream - so far so good. The cattle boy had considerately placed some bamboo poles across the worst area of mud, so I was able to teeter across without getting wet.

On the far side a group of finch-like birds were playing in the bushes, taking no notice of me, as I moved slowly and easily towards them. I got within ten feet before they took off. There were two faint tracks on the bank of the dried up stream, and I checked the sun before selecting the left one. This led through a tunnel of vegetation, where I had to stoop for more than a hundred yards - he must be a small cattle boy.

At the far end of the tunnel was another more open area, and a couple of hundred yards ahead I could see where someone had been felling the trees. I weaved my way there through the undergrowth, and came upon a set of tractor tyre marks. Since they were heading in the right direction, I followed them for some distance through a stand of sugar cane. The cane ended at another wall of jungle, where the tractor marks swung right - in the direction of the new kampong, which was not the way I wanted to go. I cast around for a while, until I spotted a faint game track heading into the jungle. On closer investigation, it emerged from a dry drainage ditch. This was about three feet deep and two feet wide. By crouching down, I could make my way along it beneath the jungle undergrowth. At least it was heading in what I reckoned to be the right direction, and there was no other alternative I could spot.

There was a bend to the right twenty yards in, where I suddenly found myself no longer alone. Coming along the drain towards me was the biggest goanna I have ever seen in Malaysia. We both stopped and stared at the same moment, no more than fifteen feet apart. He glared at me, and I glared back, while my right hand felt around slowly for a stick. This was a ticklish situation. I swear he was at least five feet long, and therefore he would have difficulty turning round in the drain, even if he wanted to. His alternative route of escape was through me - provided he wanted to escape in the first place. I suddenly stamped my right foot and yelled "YAH!" He reared up on his hind legs, scrabbled for purchase on the side of the drain, and somehow managed to jack-knife round and hightail it away from me - thank goodness.

Another twenty yards and the left side of the drain was open grass. I climbed out to find a track beside the end of a fence. Others - small people or animals - had used the same entrance or exit to the drain, because there were distinct marks diagonally up the side where I came out.

A hundred yards down the track was a kampong house, then another, followed by a group of them. The path grew into dual wheel tracks, then a gravel road, and eventually a thin strip of bitumen. Just before the start of the gravel section a man next to one of the kampong houses called to me "Mana?" which means where? or more exactly where the hell did you spring from? I told him "Oh, just walking around." He hotfooted it to the neighbours' house, where a group appeared, as he pointed at me, then back at the jungle. The bitumen widened out, and soon there were some more houses and cars around. By the time I recognised where I was, my house was less than three hundred yards away. Damned fine navigation, though I say it myself! I had been walking for an hour and a quarter, so I estimate a 6 kilometre circuit - just right for the daily walk. If I make it a habit, the spiders - and the goanna - will soon give up.

CHAPTER 14

The tenants of my JB house did not turn up as promised, and now their mobile phone is 'not yet in service' according to the recorded message. In other words it has been cut off for non-payment, since it was already in service many months ago. Then the final bill for my JB line arrived at Adam's house, with me now owing Telekom money, instead of vice versa. My tenants have run up a bill for RM906 during the time Telekom failed to cut off the line. This makes for a very serious situation.

Not only do I have no money for food etc, but by the same token I cannot go to JB and put new locks on the doors. Furthermore, I have nobody there I can trust to do it for me. In short, I'm in heaps of trouble. As I have found out over the years, entrusting such a task to a Malay is a worse bet than the horses. Otherwise I would ask Zainal to do it for me. But he has shown no recent desire to help me in any way, in spite of the fact he and his partner Adam owe me a long overdue RM10,000.

When I do have some money, a few people are in for a rude awakening. Which may be a long time in coming, since I have so far raised the spare cash to send only *Diary* 1-10 to just one solitary newspaper. The Law of Diminishing Returns has produced a result of zero Mr Smith.

On sifting through the details of my tenants' Telekom bill - in my name - I came upon two numbers which recurred quite frequently. One of them is a Mobifon number, the other is in Pasir Mas. The latter is where I caught the train to Johor Bahru, and lies between Kota Bharu and the Thai border. I went to Adam's house, where I persuaded Mrs Adam to ring the Pasir Mas number. Who should pick up the phone but Mrs tenant!

There was a long conversation before Adam's wife finally hung up. The mother is very sick, they will have money next week, will pay as soon as they receive, etc. Meanwhile, if I happen to starve to death, sorry-lah. Six days later there was still no money, so I asked Adam to try once more. At the house someone else answered, saying not here. The Mobifon continued to give the 'all lines busy' message.

I asked Adam to keep trying, and if he gets through, tell my tenants that I can no longer tolerate non-payment. If they don't have the total amount, they must pay what they have now, and make some arrangement for payment of the balance, but they cannot continue occupying my house if they pay nothing. I told Adam to say nothing about the telephone bill at this stage, until I have some money in my hand. Otherwise they might just disappear - which they may do in any case.

In the meantime they are not aware that I have the final bill. My advice to Adam if they ask where did he get their other phone numbers from, is to tell them 'this orang puteh maybe got no money, but got plenty important friends, can find out anything'. That may make the difference between them fleeing and paying.

Adam managed to spare me RM10 so I could buy enough tobacco, tea and milk to last me another few days. Then I sat down in the dumps, trying to think of something to be thankful for. Which reminded me of some of the capers in the Wild West of Papua New Guinea.

While building the large industrial estate in Lae, trouble broke out between Highlanders and Coastals - a not-infrequent occurence. This time they went a bit further than usual, burning houses and cars, looting and killing. At one stage I wanted to go to the main office via the back gravel road, since the normal one was blocked by gutted and overturned vehicles. More than halfway there I encountered another mob busy at the usual burning.

One local who knew me ran up and said "Master, better go back, big trouble." Being alone, I thought that good advice, and checked my small .22 hand gun. They had just burned down a local working men's club, simply because the man who ran it was a Highlander. He stood up in front of them, and told them since they had destroyed his business and means of livelihood, they might as well kill him. So they did, with two spears and an axe, which put an end to his problems.

I arrived back at the site as the police Mobile Unit turned up in company with Guard Dog Security - the people the company employed as security guards. The boss is a mad Aussie, who drives a semi-armoured Landcruiser, and totes his pump action shotgun everywhere. The normal route was blocked, with mobs advancing on the site looking for trouble. The alternative route, where I had just turned back, was about to be blocked also, so it was a case of be quick. We called everyone in and loaded them on the trucks - about 400 men in all. Then we formed a convoy, with the Mobile Unit front and rear, Guard Dog inside them, and the trucks in the middle. I drove one of the Nissan trucks, with the instruction "Don't stop for ANYthing." The convoy tore off along the road in a cloud of dust. The new barricade was only half formed, and our side fired a few shots in the air to keep their heads down. Most of them had already dispersed into the sugar cane on both sides of the road, from whence a shower of arrows rained upon the convoy. One arrow came through the cab of the truck, missing me by inches, then we were through and gone. *Some*thing to be thankful for?

On Sunday morning Adam arrived in a hurry. "Come on, let's go to Kota Bharu" says he. "Okay, but sit down while I have a shave, and you tell me what's suddenly so urgent."
His uncle has been admitted to hospital, and he has to go and see him, so we might as well do the hotel bit while we're there. I said okay by me, but I still want to have a good look at the hotel before I do any persuading. First port of call was the new coffe shop on the highway. The man who runs the car washing plant and repair facility is doing good business. He opened a shack for the customers who are waiting for their vehicles. Then his wife said why not make it into a coffee shop. The shack has been renovated, with a counter round two sides - and a new coffee shop is born. Adam wanted to catch a taxi, which I said I thought somewhat spendthrift all of a sudden. That comment brought forth a RM10 note for me! The taxis were all busy, and having waited quarter of an hour, I informed Adam the bus was

due any minute. The words were hardly out of my mouth when the bus hove into view, and I stuck my arm out. It was almost full, with only a few aisle seats left. Adam kindly waved me into the first one, while he went further back. This resulted in the conductor extracting the fares from me - half my RM10 gone already!

At Kota Bharu we sat in the coffee shop next to the bus station, where the friend who runs the hotel - Osman - was having a bite to eat. We sipped tea while having a preliminary discussion, then walked across the street to the hotel. At least it's in quite a good position, which is a good start. The frontage has been painted in the last year or so, and looks neat enough. Inside the front door, reception is small and cramped, with only just enough room.

Osman said he averaged 75% occupancy, and was doing quite well, which immediately made me wonder why he wanted me to help out. He went back outside while Adam and I proceeded to inspect the facilities. Adam's brother Bob - whom I already met in JB - joined us. He is trying to do some business selling tickets, but from what I could gather, not with much success.

The impression I got from my tour was that things are not as good as Osman would like us to believe. There are signs of maintenance lagging through lack of money. But that can be misleading, as many such places show similar signs in Malaysia, even when there is money available. The hotel has 24 airconditioned rooms, plus a hostel of 13 rooms on the top floor.

The hostel rooms were empty, which was the first truly pessimistic sign as far as I was concerned. Anyway, right now all they wanted me to do was see if I could bring some customers in. Meanwhile we talked all sorts of other things. Adam showed me an area downstairs which he could rent as a ticket agency. His brother said he has a friend in Kelantan State Government to ask about labour contracts - everyone has a 'friend' somewhere.

There was talk of the government carpark franchise, and even the public toilet franchise! Sometimes I weary of Adam's bright ideas, none of which ever comes off. Witness the jet skis which died, the Trooper cars which faded away, the Bakun Dam prospects which have not materialised; and most recently my chalet resort design which got him uptight - after six weeks he has not yet even had it photocopied.

I told them yes, yes, yes, but we have no money for any of those things, so what's the use of talking. Bob said he knows 'some people' in Kuala Lumpur who might put up financial backing for a decent venture. I said yes, I know those sorts of people, and all you do is work yourself to the bone for their bank balances, and finish up with nothing yourself.

My overall impression so far was that in spite of the fact Osman walks around flashing a huge wad of RM50 notes, he must be close to bankruptcy. On the other hand Adam and Bob's impression of me must be that I'm the original pessimist. I went walking round the streets in search of customers. One English couple were about to leave town; five young German

191

men were leaving tomorrow, but wished they met me three days ago; an elderly Dutch couple were quite happy where they were, but thanks very much anyway; and so on.

It was lunch time, and quite obviously the wrong time of day to be looking for customers. I had already told Adam that I should be meeting the express buses at 7 o'clock in the morning, not walking around now. But I tried in any case, just to test my own theory - I was right. I was also still worried about the hostel facilities going to waste. Many of the Europeans in town are on budget holidays, some of them complete with backpacks. The hostel is what they would be interested in. But even the hotel handout emphasises the room rates, with a search required even to discover that there ARE hostel rooms. If I was running the place, that would be the first thing I would change.

When I went back we gathered in Bob's room for discussion of a new topic. The hotel is available for rent - at RM12,000 a month complete. It took me ten minutes with pencil and paper to demolish that one. I did a rough calculation of costs and declared that RM12,000 a month simply was not on. At 70% occupancy we would go broke quite soon - even if any of us had money to rent the place. I am now Pessimist No.1 in their eyes.

Adam said Ismail was coming to pick him up and take him to the hospital at 5 o'clock. This is the same Mr. Ismail who was fire chief when I first arrived in Pasir Puteh, but was then sent to Kuala Lumpur. Now they have passed him along to Kota

Bharu as Kelantan Planning Officer. Since there was more than an hour to go before he was due, I went walking in order to find out what is within easy distance of the hotel. It's a pity about the rent price, and the lack of capital available. I'm inclined to think something might be done with it, given a lower rent and a few imaginative details. But that's life, as the corpse said to the zombie.

When Ismail turned up, we went to the restaurant round the corner for capati and tea. He and I had a bit of catching up to do, and chatted away for half an hour, with Adam hardly getting a word in. The new job is keeping him very busy so far, but at least he has a nice new government house for his family. He was looking very spruce in his pressed clothes and clipped moustache.

At the hospital, which covers a very large area, we spent ten minutes finding a parking space. We then traversed at least a kilometre of corridors to reach the ward in which Adam's uncle lay. He looked very sick, with a whole blood drip in his arm, and saline drip into his stomach. His son - Adam's cousin - and wife were already there, the wife massaging one leg, while the husband did the other.

We began chatting, and eventually Adam took over the left leg, while his cousin and I had a discussion. He recently came back from Stirling University, and now works for the State Government Water and Irrigation department. The British Government paid for his stay at Stirling University - they wouldn't pay for *my* stint. There was no such place as Stirling

University then, and I didn't qualify for a grant; my father, who contributed not one cent to my tertiary education, earned too much! Things have changed mightily since then. At that time Scotland had four universities - now they're crawling out of the woodwork wherever you look. None of that has anything to do with Adam's cousin, so he knows nothing about it. We merely discussed a wide range of subjects, finding ourselves in agreement on a surprisingly large proportion. It was half an hour later before we said our goodbyes. At one main corridor intersection Adam and Ismail went straight ahead. I said that was the wrong way, we should turn right. But they said try this way and see what's here anyway, maybe can get out nearer the car. I shrugged and tagged along. As far as I could see, there was no way through the chainlink fence between the car and the long main building. But the corridor we were following was curving back towards the far end of the main building in any case, so we shouldn't end up too far out.

When we arrived at the end of the corridor adjacent to the administration block, there was a steel gate right enough, but it was locked. Adam and Ismail turned round to retrace their steps and I said hang on a minute. Taking my house keys from my pocket, I tried the more likely looking one - and it opened the lock! Adam gave me a real funny look before he and Ismail grinned at each other. I carefully locked the gate once we were through, and it wasn't more than a short hike to the car.

Back in Pasir Puteh my tenants still did not pay the rent, with a few days left before the next payment is due. This is beyond a joke, but with very little I can do, except keep on chasing them for it. On the few occasions I have managed to talk to them, they have said they want to remain in the house, and will pay within a few days. Their idea of what constitutes 'a few' differs considerably from mine. Meanwhile, according to Zainal, their furniture is still all in the house. So at least they haven't disappeared - IF Zainal is telling the truth.

Adam came calling once more with interesting news. The hotel is owned by Kelantan State Government, and Osman has not paid the rent - of RM6,000 per month - for three months. He is prepared to vacate in our favour for RM8,000 a month - 6,000 to the government for the building, and 2,000 to him for his fittings and furnishings. Now THAT's a lot closer to cooking with gas.

Meanwhile Adam's cousin says he was most impressed by his chat with me. That's the one who was at the hospital, and whose expenses at university in my country were paid for by my government, while his wife tagged along for the ride. He has quite a bit of money put aside - why doesn't that surprise me? - and would like to invest in my cashless company with the impressive credentials. The object being to take over and operate the hotel as soon as possible. He has already put pen to paper to the State Government on the subject. All we have to do now is await a reply - which could be tomorrow, or more likely next year. That was quite uncalled for Mr. Anderson; they're slow, but not that slow. Besides which, Adam's cousin already works for the government, so there! With a modicum of good fortune I may yet have good news this side of the grave, who knows. It might even come in the shape of an envelope from a certain British newspaper, whose name not even a herd of wild horses could draw from my lips. The secret to the unsealing of my lips lies in being completely ignored for a month or two - then every wild horse would become redundant.

My JB tenants still could not be contacted, and I made up my mind to ask Franky to lock up my house with new padlocks if nothing in the next couple of days. Mrs. Adam pleaded the mother is sick, Hari Raya just over, give them a break. I said how about somebody giving me a break. I live in a cheap little kampong house while others live in my house - then don't pay the rent. She soothed my feathers by giving me RM10, since she also doesn't live in a small cheap kampong house with no tv., radio etc, while her husband owes me so much money. That will buy tobacco and food for three days. I roll my own from Dutch tobacco, one packet lasting three or four days. If I buy cigarettes they cost four times as much. Not only because they are more expensive anyway, but because I smoke more. While working at the computer, it is too easy to reach into the packet and light up another one almost unconsciously. But if you have to stop everything in order to roll one, you put it off until a more convenient time.

Adam and his wife are broke, and yet she has fed the baby on the bottle since bringing him home, even though she's quite a large woman. The cost of the milk powder is twice what I spend on tobacco and food. Even my little Liz managed breast

196

feeding for the first four months. Mind you she was a bit top heavy for a while. She weighed about 3kg over her normal 32kg or so, with most of the extra leading. Which reminds me of the doctor examining the young female patient's chest:

"Big breaths."   "Yeth, and I'm only thikthteen."

If I had enough cash to post the serial samples to a British magazine I would be much happier. The postage would only cost a week's food for one arm and leg - or maybe two legs. Which means the rest of me could still eat, so long as the arm and leg received no nourishment. Sounds as if Shylock crept into the picture - between the gallery's store room and display wall?

We are now into the hottest time of the year, having put the Monsoon behind us. Two little faces looked in the door, wanting to see the model railway. I pressed 'Save' on the computer and went through to the back room.

Having checked everything out, I switched on the power at the mains. I looked round and there were 16 little faces staring back! Twenty minutes of operation was all I could handle under the bare corrugated iron roof back there, with the sun beating down on it.   Turning my one and only fan to blow along the corridor at top speed didn't improve things much.

A month ago I was wearing a sweater in the evening. Now it's too hot to go to bed before about 1 o'clock in the morning. Yesterday evening I went outside the house for a while, and even the Man in the Moon was wearing a scowl. If I open the shutters after dark, the house fills with insects, if I shut them it's like an oven. I still have most of the mosquito mesh I bought, but I'm saving it for the beach house I was hoping to have moved into by now. Besides which, the handle of my hammer broke while attempting to remove an outsize nail from one of the window frames. Now I'm hoping a newspaper will buy this lot - and send some money - before this lousy little house and I are forced to become completely enmeshed. Which reminds me Adam still has my staple gun, and I probably now possess insufficient staples to fix all of the mesh to the frames. That's one more job nicely put off for a while longer. Given a choice between buying bread or staples, the bread wins, hands feet and bottom down. My current sustenance is rice and vegetable soup, soaked up with the cheapest local break-off-your-own-chunk bread. A few weeks longer on that diet and the rats had better be very careful. My umbrella has a strong pointed steel tip - maybe I should have been carrying it when I met the goanna in the drain.

I rang Franky's mobile phone from Adam's house with not much real hope - and got through! The Hari Raya/Chinese New Year jamming of the nation's communications system is finally subsiding. Franky was full of talk; his Director has been over from Jakarta, the Malaysian license is now fixed, soon he will have some money and be able to come and see me, got lots of new workers in Medan, his brother sick, but now gone safely back to Jogjakarta, hippity-ho, rat-a-tat-tat, what's my address now?

I gave the phone to Adam, so my ears could rest while he

recited his address and phone number - again. Then it was my turn once more. At the fifth pause for breath, I managed to squeeze in "Can I talk now?" "Oh yes, sure, go ahead. Just thought I'd bring you up to date, because you weren't very happy with me the last time we talked." I remembered being somewhat brusque when he had started looking for problems which didn't exist .I asked him if he would be prepared to go to my house and check it out. If the tenants are there, ask them to send the rent *now*. If they are not there, buy a couple of padlocks and chains, and fix it so nobody can get in until I say so. That brought a heap of questions, so I patiently explained the situation. He then asked me why I hadn't asked him to be my agent in the first place. I said I did, in a letter posted in December. Another letter he didn't receive - I thought he was just ignoring it.

CHAPTER 15

I went for my circular walk in the reverse direction today. At the dried up stream bed on the jungle section, I looked closely at the climbing vines. The two most common have flowers like sweet peas - one large and mainly blue, while the smaller-flowered one is white with blue veins. Big Sweet Pea has round glossy leaves, while Wee Sweet Pea has delicate fernlike foliage. They frequently appear together, climbing through bushes and trees.

Big Sweet Pea and Wee Sweet Pea, climbing through the bushes

Big Sweet Pea runs up ahead, Wee Sweet Pea creeps and pushesBig Sweet Pea leaps to a tree, winding through the branches

Wee Sweet Pea comes up behind, sees the gap, and blanches

Wee Sweet Pea climbs Big Sweet Pea, up closer to the clouds

Big Sweet Pea puts on a spurt - he simply can't stand crowds

There is one frequent bird call in the plantation which I have finally pinned down. It sounds like a cuckoo call in reverse, and is made by a dove-like bird, with a buff breast and grey wings. One bird I have not yet managed to clap eyes on is the one which sings sweetly in the very early hours of the morning, long before dawn. He must be quite clever, because most birds which sing as sweetly as that are already in cages around here. So far he's certainly smarter than me, which is why I haven't yet seen him.

Adam's uncle, whom we went to see in hospital, died yesterday - on his way home from the hospital. That does not inspire a feeling of confidence in the medical authorities.

A crowd of kids turned up in the afternoon to see the railway. The sun was shining, so fifteen minutes was my limit in the back room furnace. I had 2 tank engines pulling a 40-wagon train round the continuous run, while the branch passenger train shuttled to and fro. Then most of the kids sat down in the front room on the floor (not enough seats), looking through some of my books. Adam came along and had a chat, while I showed a couple of the older children how to draw pictures on the computer with 'Paintbox'.

On Monday I had intended posting *Diary* 1-10 to the 'Sunday Post', but that was not possible without money. March rent is due, and February has not yet been paid. No money, no paper for printing, no food - but plenty of 'nephews' and 'nieces' come to see the train, read books, and draw pictures on the computer.

I went to Adam's house late in the afternoon, and met another of his cousins.

Adam counts cousins
in scores and dozens.

This one is Ismail, and speaks very good English. We discussed a wide range of subjects, including the Malaysian government's current loan repayment problems, as a result of the appreciating Yen. That's what the Prime Minister wanted, and that's what he got. If he had accepted the sterling or dollar loans on offer at the time, he would have been on easy street now. But that would not have suited his 'Look East' policy.

It is only recently that it has slowly started to dawn on Malaysian politicians that Japan is busy accomplishing in Asia by economic dominance, what it could not maintain by military force.

Japanese companies with factories etc in this country make no attempt to honour their obligations to transfer technology, as their agreements stipulate. Western companies actually *do* try. On the domestic scene I ventured the opinion that most ordinary Malaysians were in danger of becoming 'slaves to the money lenders'. After he had gone, Adam told me Ismail works at Bank Bumiputera! There is an attractive new girl working at the minimarket, who makes a point of speaking to me in her broken English. Her name is Nol, and her looks are different from most of the locals. I would guess she has some Thai blood in her.

I now have not much more than a week left in which to find sufficient money to go to Golok and renew my visa. According to what I have been told, I should stay out of Malaysia for a week this time. But I dare say I'll find a way round that problem - with a little help from my lady friend at Thai Immigration. Who of course has friends at Malaysian Immigration.

Either my present tenants must pay up, or I must find new ones. But how to do that while situated in the kampong 700km away with no money? Besides which, Adam's phone has been cut off - again. So I cannot call my tenants' mobile phone, since my phonecard is also finished. Zainal called from JB to say he went to my house. There was nobody there, but their furniture is still all inside. With Franky's new padlocks and chains on the doors, that means they will *have* to contact me before they can get back inside - or take anything out while the moon is shining.

On Tuesday Adam's phone was connected again, and there was a message from my tenants. The wife has been sick with a broken rib - they had a fight, and he has left. She cannot work for a month, but will be back at work soon. On Friday she will pay February rent, followed a week later by March. That would be all very nice, but I've heard too many lies already to put my trust in her now - we shall see. Why she has to take a month off from a sedentary job because of a broken rib, I do not know. In Papua New Guinea I fell down a set of concrete shuttering, breaking one rib and cracking another. This happened at 2.30 on Saturday afternoon. I was at work at 7am Monday as usual, in spite of the pain. The worst part was driving to and from work, over roads which were more potholes than road surface.

I stayed up very late on Wednesday night, printing out samples of my writing for posting; on the off chance that my tenant might actually pay the rent on Friday as promised. By the time I finished, I had three packages ready for the off. One for a newspaper, the second for a magazine, and the third addressed to an agent.

It was 4am when I crept into bed. Unfortunately, the rats

were making too much noise in the roof, so I could not sleep. Apart from the fact that my mosquito coils are also finished, so the little fiends were divebombing me. I went back to the computer, and checked through my book *Tropical Trial*, wondering if I could afford to post some of that along with the other samples to the agent.

In the pre-dawn darkness I went walking round the kampong, before strolling out to the main road. Where I met Adam, waiting for the school bus with his daughter. As soon as the bus departed, we went to the coffee shop, where Adam bought me roti telor and teh tarik. That took care of today's food intake.

Friday passed, without a sign of my tenant, or the rent for my JB house. No rent, no money, no food in the house. Therefore once more I cannot post anything to Britain. If I can't send my writing to anyone, I certainly can't sell it. A personal experience of the vicious circle of poverty, which keeps so many people in this world permanently poor. If it's a problem for me, what hope is there for so many millions without my education and opportunity?

I had a chat with a couple of 'monkey for hire' men. The current price around the kampong is RM15 per hundred coconuts picked. In the 'city' - Pasir Puteh! - they charge RM18. The State government runs a subsidised monkey training school. A kampong man who catches a young monkey can bring it along, and they will help him train it to pick coconuts.

Zainal is supposed to go and check my house in Johor

Baru tonight. Hopefully, if Franky has placed the new padlocks as promised, my tenant will be unable to remove her furniture without contacting me first.

The weather is hot and sticky enough to be completely debilitating for the last few days. Around the kampong there is not much sign of life in the middle of the day; and my house is like an oven, even with all of the shutters open. Sunday was the hottest day yet, and I had no food in the house. But at least I had cold water in the refrigerator. My visa had only a few days left, so I had to go to Golok in Thailand for at least 3 days, no later than Wednesday. On Monday I went to see Adam, who said he had no money, and no news from my tenant. I told Adam my trip to Thailand would cost at least RM150, and I had no idea where to find the money. He said he would contact Ismail to see if he could help.

Back at the house, I disconnected the gas cylinder, and *carried* it nearly a mile to the minimarket, where I asked for a refund of my RM50 deposit. Now I cannot cook hot food; but I can make instant noodles with boiling water from the kettle - so long as the electricity is not cut off for non-payment! With the proceeds I bought cream crackers, sardines, mosquito coils and a packet of tobacco. I buy the sardines, not only because they are nutritional, but because the minimarket sells a large tin of a new brand for only RM2-00, and they are very good. Up until today I have lasted 41 days on an average expenditure of RM5-24 per day, covering food, tobacco, and everything else. Little wonder I'm so slim - much slimmer and I'll have to put an extra hole in my trousers belt.

The grapevine must have been in good shape, because an hour after my return from the shop, Adam turned up to ask what was happening. He got the message somehow that I had taken back the cylinder - which still had gas in it. He told me he had contacted Ismail, who said he would lend me RM200 to go to Thailand. While I am in Golok, Adam will get me a spare cylinder from his relatives' house in Bachok, so I can cook again. Unfortunately, Adam has an almost perfect record of not keeping promises like that, so I won't hold my breath. But Ismail is a different kettle of fish. If he says he will lend me the money, my mind is at ease. Actually, he is lending the money to Adam, to lend to me. And since Adam already owes me so much, he is the one who will have to repay it, not me.

The money arrived on Tuesday - RM50 short. I wonder if Ismail was really short of the extra fifty, or if Adam decided to deduct, since I got fifty back on the gas cylinder? That's just about the way his mind works - witness the RM300 he was short for the lorry from JB After promising he could pay it, but before I was stupid enough to open my mouth and say I had three hundred.

At 10am a Mig-29 roared low over the house at a high rate of knots, making me jump. I wouldn't have known what it was, but for the fact I glanced out through the open shutters just in time to spot it disappearing.

Mr. Ismail is to receive a medal from the Sultan this month. Another 5 years or so, and the way he is going, he will be a Datuk. I hope he makes it, since he is a great deal more deserving than many Datuks I know. I spent half of the evening preparing for my trip to Thailand.

On Wednesday morning I flagged down the 10.15am bus on the highway, and was on my way to Thailand once more. The bus was stopped at no fewer than 3 police roadblocks on the way, at 2 of which my passport was inspected. Looking at the Police Field Force personnel who man most of these roadblocks, I frequently feel uneasy. Many of them seem to be just itching to use their M16 rifles on someone. 'Trigger happy' is a phrase which springs to mind. Like so many countries in the world today, firearms - and not just sidearms - are too much in evidence around the forces of law and order for my peace of mind. It makes me wonder how many of them are properly trained in the use of their weapons - and more importantly when *not* to use them.

During the journey I noticed that the first rice crop is being harvested. It seems like only yesterday the monsoon ended, but the first fruits are already on their way to market. At the hotel in Golok I moved into my old favourite room 210, and contemplated what to do for the next 3 days. I should stay out for at least a week this time, according to what I've been told by Immigration. But sometimes I think different 'experts' tailor the regulations to suit their own interpretations. Last time here I met an attractive lady at the shop next door, who just happens to be a Thai Immigration officer. Fortunately the hotel towkay knows her, and gave me her name and address when I enquired. I had walked past the place between the border bridge and the hotel. My luck was in, as she was at home, and had not yet eaten lunch. I invited her to the coffee shop, where we both ate a fiery Tom Yam soup, thick with vegetables. By the time I finished eating, I was glancing furtively around in search of a fire engine to quench the flames.

She agreed with me that Malaysian Immigration regulations are open to interpretation by the officer on the spot, and promised to speak to her gentleman friend (boyfriend?), who just happens to be a Malaysian Immigration officer at the bridge. By Friday lunch time at the latest, she would get back to me at the hotel. I paid the lunch bill, well content with the prospect. She was on duty at 2pm, so we said goodbye for now, and I wandered back past the hotel, on my way to buy a newspaper.

On the way past, I dropped in at the shop next door for a shandy. The premises of the ladies of the night has had a face lift, and is advertising 'Barber', but the actual trade has not changed. The pavement shanty has gone, and the frontage of the building boasts a fancy new door, and a coat of fresh paint - business must be good. There is also a new stall selling local cooked dishes, between the shop and the 'Barber'. In place of the shanty there are now a couple of new stone tables and benches. Taken in conjunction with the existing ones outside the shop, we now have what is effectively a small pavement restaurant.

Shandy finished, I headed for the newspaper stall. On the

way I said hello to my lady friends at the Malay (halal) chicken stalls. Outside the second one, a small and attractive girl on a motorbike piped up 'are you alone?' I gave her a smile and a nod before continuing on my way - I'm also broke. Reading the newspaper took care of the rest of the afternoon in the hotel room.

In the evening I went to the open air Chinese restaurant, where I ate a special fried rice. While eating I was approached by a tall elegant poondang (boy/girl), who was passing with her friends. 'Papa' says she, 'you so handsome, she want make music you.' She pointed to one of her chic companions. I gave my usual smile and answered 'Not tonight thanks, I'm on a diet.'

I spun out my shandy with plenty of ice, watching the world go by, until it was time for bed. The place was not too busy, so my usual Chinese waitress managed to sit and chat between customers. She is very attractive, and pleasant to chat with.

On Thursday I was buying lunch at the Malay chicken stall, when the petite Indian lady beggar came along. She is very small and pretty beneath the poor clothes, and carries a child of about two and a half. Last time in town I gave her some coins at the Chinese restaurant. But I couldn't help wondering if maybe she was up to the Bombay Bludge - hire a kid for the day and go begging. I spent some time in Bombay - 3 times actually - and am well aware of most of the scams. If the kid doesn't know how to act properly, give it a pinch now and again to make it cry.

The child was a girl, with enormous eyes, and pensive expression, and at least it was still the same child as before. But this time, since I was at the stall anyway, I decided not to give money. Instead I ordered 2 extra chicken legs with trimmings. When I handed them over, the young lady and the child did seem to be genuinely hungry, and showed signs of gratitude - so maybe they are not pseudo beggars after all, but the real thing. It's a sad old world sometimes.

Another horrendous bus smash in Thailand yesterday. Only the worst make the newspapers, or they would contain nothing else. Which is why I am averse to taking a bus anywhere in the country. Malaysia is bad enough, with the lack of organized enforcement of road rules. You are about 3 times as likely to be killed on the roads in Malaysia as you are in Britain. In Thailand the risk doubles again, so why push your luck?

On Friday morning, following breakfast at the roti canai shop, I took my newspaper to the Malay coffee shop in town, where I have occasionally had teh tarik in the past. The teh tarik at the roti canai shop is frequently well stewed, whereas at the coffee shop it is always fresh and fragrant.

The coffee shop man immediately told me it was about 2 months since he had seen me, welcome back - he must have a very good memory. Playing around outside the shop were 3 kids, the eldest on roller blades. He was 10 years old, with a girl of 8 and another boy 5. They looked like brothers and sister, and gravitated to my table. For some time we conversed via sign language and drawings. The older boy was quite an artist with my pen and paper, bringing forth a few smiles with his caricatures. One of which depicted me throwing a perfectly good cigarette into a waste basket. He kept up the pressure throughout most of the time I spent in the coffee shop. No danger of him taking up smoking - for now at any rate. Meanwhile the girl and I exchanged funny faces, and the small boy kept wanting to sit on my lap. I submitted to his entreaties in the end, and played a few rounds of 'round and round the garden', which brought squeals, giggles and wriggles.

Then it was time for my famous spider act. This comprises my left hand 'walking' and darting across the table top like a spider (I have 'piano fingers'), until swatted by my right hand. The spider then flips upside down, wiggles its legs in the air, and falls off the edge of the table. They soon cottoned on, and there was a competition to see who could swat the spider first, as it darted around the table top - after all impediments had been removed to the next table.

When the spider was starting to smart - they were trying hard to kill it - I bought them a banana each, to take the pressure off. My teh tarik returned to the table, barring further spider excursions for a while. The older boy went back to his one-man anti-smoking campaign as soon as I lit up, but his sister came to my defence. I'm not sure that was a good thing, but I'm not yet ready to give up the noxious weed.

With my second teh tarik glass empty, I checked the time - I had been playing with the kids for two hours! Saying goodbye

211

was no simple matter. The five-year-old wouldn't let go of my hand, and the girl had a long sad face, with a trace of tears in her eyes. One of the coffee shop ladies came to take the little one, and I gave them 10bht each. That seemed to brighten things up - maybe that's what the little bludgers were up to all the time? I don't like to think so, since I'm a natural romantic at heart.

The older boy followed me halfway back to the hotel on his roller blades, before saying his tenth and final goodbye - accompanied by a pantomime of throwing my latest cigarette in the nearest rubbish bin. My lady Immigration friend was waiting for me at the pavement cafe, which worried me. But she assured me she had just arrived a few minutes before me. I took her to the restaurant across the street, where I was careful to select the least fiery dish for myself, while she happily scoffed the hottest. She informed me that her friend was on duty tomorrow morning, and would help me. Could I contribute RM10 towards his coffee money? I said I certainly could, what about herself? She said she wanted nothing for herself, except maybe I could take her to lunch sometimes when I'm in town? This was said with some deference, and I hastened to reassure her that I would be happy to oblige, as I enjoy her company. She speaks passable English, and is an intelligent woman. I suspect most Thai men don't bother to indulge in intelligent conversation with women.

I managed to pass the RM10 over without drawing attention, and she told me the 'form'. Tomorrow morning at

11am, I pass through Immigration at the Malaysian end of the bridge. I must go to the left window, where her friend Mr.-- will be on duty. He will be wearing a name tag, so make sure it's him before presenting my passport, and he will give me a 2-month visa. She assured me there is nothing illegal in it, since it is within his authority, and technically I am not offering him any money. Sounded good to me, so long as I get the visa.

Later I was reading the newspaper (Malaysian) in the room, having had no opportunity at the coffee shop. Yesterday in Malaysia there was another 'shoot out' between a gang of 'suspected' robbers and the police. During which, as appears to have become quite normal, all 11 members of the gang were shot dead, while - again as usual - not a single policeman was harmed. In fact the last time I recall reading of a policeman being shot, it was another policeman who fired the bullet.

There seems to be a disturbing amount of 'overkill' on the part of the police in recent months. They seem to open up with rifles, assault weapons etc at the slightest provocation. And the shooting appears to continue until the ammunition - or at the very least, the magazine - is spent. I don't know whether it's simply a case of poor training, combined with a 'trigger happy' mentality from watching too many Hollywood movies - or something altogether more sinister. I know for a fact that orders are sometimes issued in Indonesia for police to 'get rid of' criminals rather than bring them in, but I didn't until now suspect that it might happen in Malaysia. Lately I have begun to wonder about that.

CHAPTER 16

I sat in the hotel room on Friday evening, thinking about the police 'shoot outs' and other anomalies I have come across. The government of Malaysia has a habit of suppressing unpleasant facts it would rather people didn't know about. For instance, Malaysian fishermen are constantly harassed by Indonesian patrol boats, in Malaysian waters as well as international. The Indonesians demand money and valuables, and if they don't get them, they destroy the fishermen's nets. Sometimes they even hijack the boats and take them to Indonesia, with a trumped up story of smuggling or such like.

When the fishermen complain to the authorities in Malaysia, they are more often than not told to stop 'making trouble'. This is not mere hearsay, or secondhand information - I have spoken personally to many of the fishermen who have been looted. But the Malaysian government would rather ignore the situation than 'offend' their big neighbour. Official government statements deny the existence of piracy in the Straits of Malacca. They even hold joint 'security' exercises in the Malacca Strait every now and again. I've spoken to navy personnel who have taken part in those exercises - I used to be an honorary member of the Petty Officers' Mess, as well as the Navy Yacht Club, at the main Malaysian Navy base in Lumut. Many of them seem to think it's a great joke on the Malaysian public to sail around playing cops with some of the robbers.

Yesterday a man was arrested outside a Malaysian jail,

after completing his one year sentence. He has been charged with no crime, but instead has been arrested under the Internal Security Act. This and the Emergency Ordinance Act are constantly used by the police when they have nothing else they can produce. They can then hold people without having to try them in a proper court. Every week there are cases of people being acquitted by a court, only to be re-arrested outside the court under one of those iniquitous Acts.

Freedom of religious expression is supposedly engraved in the Malaysian Constitution. But every Malay has to be Moslem from birth, like it or not. And it is the official government-approved version of Islam to which they must subscribe. Anyone who teaches a different version of Islam is liable to be imprisoned. Recently there was a deviant sect who were hassled, arrested, and eventually sent for 're-education' in the 'proper' version of Islam. Then there is the case of Myanmar - which I still prefer to call Burma - versus Bosnia, as a further instance. The Malaysian government accuses European governments and the U.N. of being hypocrites for not going in and massacring Serbs in Bosnia. Meanwhile, on their back doorstep, the military regime of Burma goes about its daily round of killing, raping and looting. Malaysian politicians say this should be handled by means of 'constructive engagement' in co-operation with its ASEAN allies.

This is the very policy for which those same politicians so vehemently criticised Britain and the U.S. when they applied it to South Africa. Who then is more hypocritical than whom?

The Prime Minister of Malaysia refused to attend the fiftieth birthday celebration of the United Nations because of his interpretation of the situation in Bosnia. He has made it a convention for people in this part of the world to denigrate the U.N. The fact is that, without the U.N. the world as a whole, and the Third World in particular, would be a lot worse off.

Under the U.N. widespread diseases have been controlled, and in some cases eradicated. Millions of people have been saved from starvation and death. Millions more who had no drinking water, now have it. These, and other achievements, are what the world should celebrate; instead of censuring the U.N. because it is unwarlike. It was not the intention of the founding fathers of the U.N. that it should indulge in armed conflict. It is supposed to be a humanitarian organization, and if it is to learn the craft of war, it needs time to do so. Better to hand warlike functions to those more capable of carrying them out, as in Korea, and Bosnia - if you *must* indulge.

Those who say the U.N. is of no use are simply demonstrating to the world their own myopic and selfish point of view. Of course the U.N. needs re-organizing. Of course it has shortcomings. No such organization run by mortals can ever be anywhere near perfect. But to state - as many have - that it is of no use, and should be scrapped, is to deny mankind its greatest hope. You might as well try to stop your baby from learning to walk, on the basis that he keeps falling over. Then refuse to attend his birthday party because of his falls.

A world democratic body cannot possibly please

everyone all of the time. The most it can hope to achieve is to please a majority of its members most of the time. True democracy is based on the greatest good for the greatest number. Minority opinions will always suffer under *any* system. Democracy must simply make sympathetic allowance for those minorities, without bending to their will.

I am the first to admit this is something most Western societies seem to have forgotten, with politicians constantly chasing minority pressure group votes which may hold a balance of power. But as Winston Churchill said 'I beg you always to remember that democracy is the worst possible form of government - except for all the rest.'

It is also much more honourable and decent to have tried and failed, than not to have bothered trying in the first place. Jeez, I do get on my high horse sometimes, don't I?

I figured out how many samples of my writing I could afford to send out, if my tenant has paid the rent when I return to Pasir Puteh.......

I sit in the hotel room, writing down how much money I have, what I can and cannot afford. Wondering whether I should dump the rent and electricity accounts on Adam and hightail it out of Kelantan; and knowing very well I will do no such thing. Personal honesty and decency can have a dire effect on one's living conditions at times. Mind you, my current Bible is stamped on the front, *Placed by the Gideons*, so I'm no saint!

I thought briefly of blowing some of the money on a night or two out on the town, but that doesn't appear too wise right now. No Andaman Cafe, no Nas. I cannot bring myself to start something new. That little bitch of a wife of mine has me for the rest of my life – or hers. Betrayal or not, coma or otherwise, I cannot bring myself to abandon her now. In spite of the fact she abandoned me first. In short I still love her. I must have a masochistic streak somewhere in me. Committing the rest of my life to her care will surely keep me poor financially. On the other hand, there may be some reward spiritually - or more likely not.

Thoughts of reward are in any case only selfishness. Better to get on with finding a way of saving enough money to bring her back where she belongs. If I could raise the money to send samples of my writing to enough people, I'm sure I can sell at least some of it. If not, it has been one hell of a long expensive and painful experience for less than nothing. In the meantime there's still hope of convincing Singapore Airlines to get Liz back to Singapore using some of the money in her CPF account.

It is difficult to figure out what way to go about resolving my current dilemma. Advice varies from 'divorce and find another' to 'convert to Islam, and can have one more without divorcing this one'. The first I cannot yet bring myself to do, and I don't think I ever will now. The second may appear easy at first glance, but one thing I have tried never to be is a hypocrite. I have always tried to be a good Christian. Not so much a public church-on-Sunday Christian - though I was once a bible class teacher - but more in the way I live my daily life according to basic beliefs.

My religion is a quiet affair between me and God, and simply obliges me to make a conscious effort at all times not to harm others. It does not require a public display of worship to prove to others how good or pious I am. In fact, that would be the facet of Islam most offensive to me. Otherwise the God of Islam, Christianity and Jewry is really one and the same God. It is therefore truly a human tragedy that so many people have died - and go on dying - in the name of the different interpretations - by humans - of what is basically the same religion. The term 'Holy War' is a complete contradiction in terms. How can any religious leader of any denomination call on the blessing of the Almighty Father in pursuit of the slaughter of others of His children? The trouble with most organized religions is that the ambitious politicians in mufti end up running the show *their* way.

Converting to Islam would be the easy way out for me, but I always seem to opt for the difficult paths in life. Not only because I'm stubborn and pigheaded, though that's a fair part of it. But because by opting for the more difficult path, I have so far lived a truly interesting life. On my death bed I will at least have the consolation of knowing I have done my best to truly live, as opposed to merely existing.

George Stephenson put it rather well - "I have dined with princes, peers, and commoners, with persons of all classes, from the humblest to the highest. I have dined off a red herring when seated in a hedge-bottom, and I have gone through the meanest drudgery. I have seen mankind in all its phases, and

the conclusion I have arrived at is this - that if we are stripped,
there is not much difference."

None of which contributes one iota to the solution of my dilemma. Advice from friends, relatives etc is all very well, and no doubt given with the best intent. But in all truth, very few people are qualified to give advice in such a situation. In the end I know I will do what my conscience permits, no more or less.

In an ideal world, I would be able to make enough money from writing to rent a big house where housing is cheap - Indonesia for instance. There I would be able to train maybe 3 widows or abandoned wives to help me care for my wife, instead of leaving her in hospital or nursing home. They in turn would receive free board and lodging plus local wage rate, instead of being out on the street. I could sit at the computer upstairs overlooking the sea; writing my books while still able to keep an eye on my wife. Take her down to the beach sometimes, no matter how difficult that might be - where there's a will there's a way. Being the stubborn person I am, I feel that, in spite of what doctors say, maybe loving care can achieve what they cannot. It's certainly worth a try.

I'll continue on short rations, in order to send samples to as many people as possible, until I get a result. Waiting 2 months for a reply before sending to someone else just is not working out. Not that I've had money to do much more anyway. But if I can find a new tenant, then I'll send as much as I can, and worry about eating later. They say you have to be at least a little mad to be a writer. I think on that basis I must surely qualify by now.

On Saturday morning I miss-timed things slightly, in my eagerness to be on time at the Malaysian end of the bridge. I therefore spent ten minutes standing in the middle of the bridge, smoking a cigarette, and watching life on the river. It's quite amusing to watch the sampans ferry people across the narrow waterway, without benefit of passport or Immigration procedures - within a hundred metres of the Immigration checkpoints. While I worry about my visa.

Adam told me before that if I had a problem, his friends would help me out. I have the mobile phone number of his big-time 'friend' here in Rantau Panjang, who would arrange things for me free. But he moved from Sarawak because of police trouble there. Then he moved from Johor Baru to Rantau Panjang for the same reason. Using him would just as likely get *me* into police trouble. For all I know he might be on the verge of having to move once more. Better to make my own arrangements, if and when necessary. Having studied the problem, it would really be quite easy to resolve. The main stumbling block would be the police roadblocks. Which simply means I would take the long way round by private car or taxi. It's only while in a bus that my passport has ever been checked at a roadblock - and I've been through some hundreds of them in this country over the years.

I took my time filling in the arrival card, and finally presented it to the smiling gent behind the left counter window at exactly 11am. "Welcome back to Malaysia Mister Anderson" said he, as he chopped my passport with a 2 month visa, accompanied by another broad smile. "Thank*you*" said I with a smile of my own, and the problem was resolved for a further 2 months.

In Pasir Puteh there was no good news of any sort awaiting my return. I checked my remaining meagre funds, and decided there was enough to send one lot of samples to Britain. I *must* send at least one lot to a literary agent, or I cannot hope to sell anything - whether I eat or not in the meantime.

I bought 3 pads of 50 sheets each of typing paper at the minimarket for RM4.50, and prayed that the ink cartridge in the printer would hold out long enough to print out all of *'Agents.M'* from the computer. This comprises various samples of my works, plus personal resume and synopses of all my writings. Unfortunately, in original form it comprises just over 200 pages. I spent a couple of hours chopping and changing until I had it down to less than 150 pages. Then I carefully tore out every sheet individually from the pads, and fed them into the printer right way round. It was late in the evening by the time I had everything in the large addressed envelope ready to go. Each page had to be set up separately. Then of course the stupid dumb computer has to memorize the entire document every time, in order to print a single page. The printer then waits as it scans from the beginning - every single time. But right now, time is the only thing I have available to spend in lavish quantities. If I told it to print 50 pages at a time, I would almost certainly have a series of paper jams, because one end of each sheet has gum on it from the pad binding. That would waste paper and ink - neither of which I can afford.

On Saturday morning the weather was decidedly unsettled, with squally showers. I couldn't take the chance of getting my big envelope wet, so I watched and waited. At 1 o'clock I took advantage of what looked like a large enough break in the weather. Out on the highway I caught a taxi within five minutes, and was safely inside the post office ten minutes later - waiting in the usual queue. When it was finally my turn, the lady put my envelope on the scales, fiddled with her calculator, and said

"Twenty eight ringgit please." Since I had a grand total of RM30.50 left to my name, I said in Malay "Could you weigh it again please? Britain far enough, I don't want to send this one to the moon." The man behind me giggled, but the post office lady scowled and said "Twenty eight ringgit", so I parted with the funds.

Outside I decided to walk the 6 kilometres or so to my kampong house. Five packets of instant noodles cost RM2.20 and I had RM2.50 - me take taxi, no money left for mee. Two days' tariff on a Thai hotel room is a lot to pay for a single letter.

Halfway back the big thunderstorm caught me. The wind was gusting so strongly, I had to close my umbrella. I arrived home thoroughly soaked, which is not such a tragedy in this climate - my skin is waterproof. Having stripped and towelled off - no need to bathe again - I contemplated my predicament. With a shrug I decided what the hell, somebody will come up with

223

enough money for me to go to JB and sort out my house, if I put sufficient pressure on Adam.

Monday morning I went to Adam's house, to explain my position in detail - after eating the second packet of instant noodles. I put them in my large enamel mug, pour boiling water on from the kettle, put the lid on the mug, and ten minutes later they are fit to eat. The instructions say you are supposed to boil them for at least two minutes, but my way works perfectly well - and I have no gas with which to cook.

Adam doesn't even look like getting me the cylinder he promised to get from Bachok while I was in Golok. But that's par for the course with Adam, so I never counted on it in the first place. Maybe tomorrow will bring more hope - maybe not. Adam told me Haji Hussein from Johor Baru was at his house while I was in Thailand. He is coming back tonight or tomorrow morning. I told Adam that in my opinion, Haji would not be back if he knows I am here. He is just one more of a long line of Malay gentlemen who have cheated me, and owe me money.

Adam said 'No, no, he was actually looking for you in JB He has a good land deal going here, and I am acting as agent for a hundred acres of development land. Please don't say anything about the money he owes you." I told him I wouldn't have to, because Haji would not turn up.

On Tuesday it rained most of the day, and I ate the third packet of mee. As I had predicted, Haji Hussein did not turn up. When I returned from the toilet, a chitchat was calmly drinking the last of my Ovaltine from the mug. He glanced up at me, then

224

finished quenching his thirst before darting behind the computer.

Sometimes, when I have forgotten to put the mug in the kitchen sink at night, the dregs of Ovaltine are gone, and the mug licked clean in the morning. Ovaltine is a part of the chitchat diet you won't find in the biology books. But that's the last of it for now, so we'll both have to change our diet.

Wednesday dawned fine and sunny, so I got on with washing all of my bedding. It was dry and back on the bed by the time the rain returned before noon. Zainal was at Adam's house when I went there, but avoided talking to me; until I cornered him in the lounge. He confirmed that he went to my house, and my tenant's furniture is still all inside. Unfortunately I don't believe much that Zainal tells me nowadays. Adam gave me RM10 as I was leaving, so I went straight to the shop and bought tobacco, sardines and cream cracker biscuits. I buy the biscuits because they are better value than the bread.

That means I now have enough supplies to last until Friday. Adam said Haji Hussein went straight back to Johor Baru on urgent business, but will be back next week. Not while I'm here, I thought. But if I'm wrong, I can go back to JB with him. Zainal has no intention of offering me a lift, though he is well aware of my position, and he is jointly responsible for my unpaid RM10,000.

By bed time I had scoffed the entire large tin of sardines, and more than half the biscuits - I was hungry. Thursday morning I was still hungry, so I scoffed the remaining rations. Now I'll just have to pretend to be a camel until the next lot of food puts in an appearance, from goodness knows where. There were piles of magnificent black thunder clouds going all round us, without a single drop of rain touching us in the middle. The usual crowd of kids had their hour of watching the trains. I don't know if any of them actually stayed for the whole hour, as there were several batches, and I didn't keep track.

On Friday morning it occured to me that I have enough rail to make a second circuit. No sooner said than done - I spent the morning doubling the track around the room. At least when I'm busy with the railway, I forget to be hungry. By the time the new circuit was complete, I had lost another gallon of sweat under the sun-drenched iron roof. Just as I was drinking the first quart of sweat replacement, the gang turned up. I told them renovations underway, come back when the sun goes down. I went to Adam's house twice in the afternoon, but nobody home - I'd hoped to scrounge some money, or at least some food. Saturday was hot and sunny - and there was a power cut. I sat on my big wooden crate outside the front door, drinking cold water, and watching the kampong activity. That was a bit too much like watching the grass grow, so I went for the circular walk.

So much for Adam getting me another gas cylinder from Bachok while I was in Thailand - I've been back a week, and there's no sign of it. But as I said when he made the promise, I won't hold my breath.

By 'lunch' time on Sunday I was feeling more than a little peckish, and visited Adam's empty house three times. I then sat in my house contemplating whether to ask Ahmad for a loan; but I'm not yet that desperate. As I was thinking this, I was looking straight at the man himself, feeding the chickens. He looked up and waved me to come over. In his house, I sat sipping rose water, while he quizzed me over Adam. He must have received some information from somewhere, because his questions were quite pointed. I told him the story from the beginning, with a tailpiece to the effect that I am not at all happy with recent developments. He didn't offer any money, and I didn't ask. But he did give me a few jambu fruit off his tree, which soothed the hunger pangs a little. A check of my stores revealed that there was some rice left, as well as half a packet of curry powder. I removed the burner from the gas stove, and replaced it with a couple of sawn-off candles. An hour later I had a bowl of most forgettable 'curry rice'.

On Monday morning I went to Adam's house in a bad mood. Adam spouted his usual 'no money', to which I replied with a few carefully chosen epithets. I stalked off in high dudgeon, and was already outside his gate when he called me back. He had 'just found' ten ringgit he 'didn't know' he had.

CHAPTER 17

With Adam's RM10 I bought the usual tobacco and Maggi Mee. This time was more mee, and cheap and nasty local tobacco. I still have a school instrument case full of Tally Ho cigarette papers I brought back from Papua New Guinea.

Mohan came calling on his bike in the afternoon. He wants to give Franky another go, and this time I do the talking. He says it was S.U.K. who gave the previous contract away to someone else, not him. That only confirms what I thought. We went to his house and called Franky, who said he would come 'straight away' as soon as he had transport.

Ten minutes after my return from Mohan's house, Adam turned up, with rather a hangdog expression. He says he can raise enough money for me to go to JB by the weekend, and sort out my house. I told him if he has any problem, to put up my television as security. That's the big one from PNG which is quoted at RM150 to fix. It was only used for 6 months before it played up, and even at half price it's worth RM600.

Tuesday was another stinking hot day, with no visitors. I spent most of the day in the 'carport' reading - for the fifth time? - *River God* by Wilbur Smith. I find something new each time I read this fascinating book. Just as well, because among my heap of books, there is not one I haven't read at least twice.

On Wednesday Adam came calling once more, with a couple of bills for me - Telecom and Company Secretary. They would have to be the least of my worries right now. The postman passed by an hour later, which means they weren't delivered today!

After buying the Kelantan tobacco, I cut a couple of slices of Ahmad's jambu fruit, and put them in a plastic bag with some of the Kelantan tobacco. In the hope that the fragrance and moisture exchange might make the tobacco less unpleasant to smoke - it did!

The weather was so hot and sticky, I spent the night working at the computer, then went for my walk. This was started before dawn, and completed in daylight. I then decided it was cool enough to sleep, and turned in, with the fan going full blast. I was just dropping off when Mohan knocked on the door and called loudly for me. There is a problem with Franky - why else would he come to my house so early?

I splashed my face, dressed, and went to Mohan's house, where I rang Franky. Franky has been caught up in the illegal settlements issue, which has been big in the newspapers recently. He must move out immediately, and has not yet found alternative accommodation. I told him that whatever his problems, he must be here by Tuesday, or don't bother talking to me about labour supply any more. If he has nowhere before then, he can leave his wife in my house until his return. Also, I will go back to JB with him when we have concluded the business. Always provided Adam comes up with the money promised 'by the weekend'.

By the time I eventually returned home, it was too hot to sleep, so I sat in the shade outside, and read *The Fraternity of*

The Stone by David Morrell, for the ? time. I usually hang onto such books, until I have too many for the space available. Then I go looking for a charity to donate them to. Before leaving Australia for Singapore, I gave away 3 crates full to The Smith Family. It took 4 men to carry each one out to the truck. But it was worth their trip, as there was a lot of other quite good linen, clothing, kitchenware etc as well.

We moved house - almost literally - at the time. I even made enquiries for a container to take the Trans Am as well - until I found out the Road Tax cost for such a beast in Singapore. One month's tax on the Trans Am was enough to buy a very second-hand Ford Cortina station sedan! That's why Singapore people just do not buy cars with 7 litre engines. They had to extrapolate the cost, because it was off their graph. The tax cost per cc rises with the number of ccs, so a 7 litre engine costs a great deal more than 7 x 1litre engines.

Friday brought the return of my manuscript sample from *The People's Friend* in Scotland, together with covering letter. They enjoyed reading it, but in its current form it is not suitable for the magazine. There was a pamphlet enclosed *Writing for the Friend*. I see what they mean, as the magazine has changed very much since I used to read it many years ago. Now it seems to be aimed at women who find their kids under cabbage leaves in the vegetable garden. Sour grapes talking? At least they went to the trouble of sending everything back at their expense, since I had no money for return postage. Thanks *Friend*, even if you didn't want it - it's nice to hear from *Some*body in the outside world, especially when they show some old-fashioned courtesy. Now I have to scrape up enough money to send samples to another magazine, and goodness knows how long that will take. My crystal ball gave up the ghost long ago.

On Saturday evening Adam's daughter turned up at my door, bearing a container of delicious Kelantan laksa. Accompanied by a gaggle of friends come to watch the model railway for a while - fair exchange! If they all brought little gifts of food, I wouldn't have to buy any. Mind you, if they *all* did, I wouldn't have enough storage room.

Sunday was hot and quiet. Ahmad popped over for fifteen minutes, bearing jambu fruits - and the rumour that the bus agency run by Adam and Zainal has gone bankrupt. On Monday morning the rumour was confirmed - I went to Adam's place and asked straight out. That's why Zainal has been here for so long this time. If he goes back to JB someone will probably take the car, and maybe his shirt as well. The way they do things, God only knows how many moneylenders they are already into - besides me! Now what to do? Adam now says it will be 'maybe a month or two' before he can raise the money for the truck to JB.

I resolved to send my tenants in JB written notice to vacate as soon as the rent reaches two months overdue. There is no sense in me remaining here if they don't pay the rent *and* run up a big phone bill on *my* phone. I might as well live in comfort in my own master bedroom, and find a tenant to rent the other bedrooms while sharing the facilities. We can have one toilet each and share the kitchen. They can have the lounge, I don't really need it.

A few days later Ahmad brought Noordin the village school teacher to see me. I had noticed her passing by a few times on her small motorcycle, and wondered who she was. She usually managed a smile and a wave, but had never stopped to chat.

She wondered if I could help her with some of the school papers, as they had no computer or printer. She was a slim attractive woman in her early thirties. Ahmad told me her husband was lost at sea in the tragic sinking of the *KD Sri Perak* patrol boat in 1984, only weeks after their marriage. I remember discussing that sinking with the Admiral, at the Lumut Yacht Club, a year after the event. One of the young officers partially responsible for the accident – he'd been asleep on duty - was dating the singer at the bar in Sitiawan in which I had a minority share. When I mentioned his name to Noordin, she didn't want to talk about him.

When I had asked the Admiral why the young officer only lost 6 months seniority, his answer was a beauty. "If we discharged every young officer who made a mistake, we wouldn't have any left." I guessed the teaching profession gave Noordin the contact she needed with children. Apparently she had loved her husband very much, and had no desire to re-marry.

For the next few weeks she called on a daily basis, bringing drafts of what she needed me to produce. At first I was embarrassed at what might happen when I ran out of paper and/or ink for the printer. But I needn't have worried. Before either ran out, she supplied new ones, without asking. Usually it took only about ten minutes to go over her requirements, but she often stayed an extra half hour or so. She liked to ask about the places I had been, and what I had done around the world. On other occasions we would discuss the difference between the rigid attitude of the Mentri Besar of Kelantan, and the more tolerant way of Islam practiced by most of the State's population. I enjoyed our little chats, and was always sorry to see her leave. She shone a little light into my loneliness. She also more often than not brought me some of her home cooking!

At first I produced simple test papers in Malay. Then came the gradings and overall performance figures, and finally the actual term examination papers. In between I produced roll-call lists for attendance purposes, and even details of the school budget! I soon became familiar with most of the names of the schoolchildren. Many of the ones who came to see the model railway were in her class, and it was interesting to put faces to the names. Of course everything is in Malaysian, so My Bahasa Melayu is still improving.

As exam time came closer my house became more frequently crowded with kids competing for my encyclopedias and my huge 552-page Rand McNally world atlas. In spite of its size and weight, I have carted that atlas from Australia to Singapore, Malaysia, PNG, and back to Malaysia.

By the time the exams were over my situation was

becoming really desperate. One month's rental had been paid in the interim on my JB house, but the rent was now once more two months behind. I told Adam I would have to vacate the kampong house and take all my belongings back to JB as soon as possible. He should get a message to my tenant via Zainal that she is to vacate because I'm taking my house back. Adam said he could arrange for one of his friends to take my furniture to JB in his truck. I told him I would go with the furniture, and save train fare!

It was another week before the truck – and Adam's money - was available, then as usual I had to do most of the hard work loading my goods. By 6pm all was ready for the trip, and I said goodbye to my little yellow kampong house. It took a little longer to say goodbye to my friends. A large part of the kampong population seemed to have turned up to wish me well. After half an hour of shaking of hands and hugging, we were finally on our way.

The truck cab wasn't too bad for room, with driver, offsider and myself inside. Unfortunately my side of the seat next to the window had long since given up its stuffing, which been replaced by a sheet of plywood. By the time we reached JB I had a numb bum. In the meantime we motored through the night, stopping every now and then for fuel and refreshments. Less than an hour into the journey the offsider – who actually owned the truck - started to tell me they were doing the trip far too cheaply, and I should really pay more. I had visions of being dumped in the middle of nowhere, so I started talking seriously.

By the time I had finished detailing my predicament, the sins of my tenant, and describing the position of my poor little wife, he had tears in his eyes, and there was no more talk of extra payment.

I paid for refreshments at the first stop, from my meager supply of money. After that the owner insisted on taking turns to pay, and they were really quite nice people. We had a two-hour break in the early hours of the morning on the outskirts of Kuantan. The truck owner had some relatives he wanted to visit, so the driver had a nap in the cab, while I went for a walk. It didn't seem like a very palatable or scenic neighbourhood, with rundown small businesses scattered here and there among emaciated trees.

I persevered, and soon came to a rubber plantation. It was not yet dawn, but a half moon was giving a fair amount of light. The rubber tappers were out, as the pre-dawn hours are the best for tapping. A slim and gracious Indian lady tapper of indeterminate age invited me to have tea and chapatti with her and her husband on the front porch of their little house. I've found that with Indian women, the poor ones are the most gracious. As soon as they get rich, most of them also get fat – it seems to be a status symbol.

She was the tapper, but had seen me as a good excuse for a break. Her husband was a 'monkey for hire' man. I told them about my rice farmer friends in Kelantan, and that broke the ice nicely. We were soon chatting about a dozen different things, and time flew. When I checked my watch, I was already overdue back at the truck. I bade a hasty farewell, and ran (trotted more like) to where the truck was parked 2 kilometres away. The driver was awake and said he was about to come and look for me. I wasn't late after all, because it was another fifteen minutes before the boss turned up.

Some time after dawn, in a small coastal village in Johor, the truck hit a dog. I expected the driver to stop, but the owner said no way. If we stopped there would be haggling over the dog, which would surely be the best dog in Malaysia, and worth a fortune. Instead of stopping we speeded up.

We arrived at my house in Taman Johor Jaya at about 9am. Franky was there, as I had rung him before leaving the kampong. He informed me that my tenant was still inside, but refused to open the door. She also had a couple of large local male 'friends' with her. This seemed to call for some diplomatic negotiation, so I banged on the steel security door and shouted "Come out of my house!"

I was not in the best of moods. First thing I had done was check the mailbox at the front gate. There was a Final Warning from Elcom to pay the electricity bill – of RM845 – or be disconnected. That was the final straw, on top of two months rent and a phone bill nearing RM1,000. Her big friends opened the door a crack and made threatening noises and gestures. Just in case she had lied to them – which was an odds-on bet – I listed her sins for their consideration. I also showed them the electricity bill, unpaid for 5 months. That resulted in some uncertainty on their part.

They agreed to come outside and negotiate. 'My' truck had a half load to go back to Kelantan. The owner told her he would give her a special rate to take her and her goods with him. Provided she was ready to load by noon. She told him her brother would pay him when they arrived in Kelantan. I said I wanted some kind of guarantee for at least *some* of the money she owes me. She was only interested in making promises, and I already knew how little they were worth. She was quite a good actress, and played everyone for as much sympathy as she could get. It had no effect on me, but Franky seemed to be drawn in, and tried to persude me to be nice to her!

Eventually we started unloading my stuff and getting it inside, after pushing my Mini van over to one side, via a series of zig-zags. The battery was flat and the tyres soft, but everything else seemed present and correct. I had wanted to drive it to Kelantan when I rented out the house, but it had a habit of overheating after less than an hour on the road. My local garage tried to fix it 3 times without success. Now the road tax has expired, so I'll have to try and persuade Zainal to get me one of his El Cheapo road tax stickers.

My tenant and her friends began shifting her stuff into the front carport. Just as well I have wide French doors in front. It didn't take long to get all my stuff off the truck, because the owner was in a hurry to pick up his half load in town. So he and the driver got stuck in with me, instead of letting me do it all. There was busy two-way traffic through the French doors for a while. The truck departed as soon as all was unloaded.

I told my tenant I was going to keep her automatic washing machine to help pay her unpaid electricity bill, at which she kicked up a hell of a wail. We had a fair old argument about it, with her threatening to call her 'friend' in the police. I told her the washing machine was worth less than the bill, and she still owed two months rent. On top of that there was the phone bill for a thousand Ringgit. So if she kept arguing, I would keep more than the washing machine. She rattled off something in dialect to her Kelantan friends, who promptly disappeared out the gate.

Half an hour later they returned in a police car, with a sergeant and constable. The sergeant proceeded to tell me that what I proposed to do was illegal, and if I tried to keep the washing machine, or any other of my tenant's property, I would be charged with stealing! I argued with him, and asked the name of his inspector, which he refused to give. I then looked around for support from Franky, only to discover that Franky had disappeared. After a further fifteen minutes of dispute with the sergeant, the mystery of Franky's disappearance was solved. He had finally decided whose side he was on. A larger police car parked at the gate, complete with Franky – and the area police superintendent!

The latter quickly queried the sergeant's business here, and told him to go about his lawful business – the dispute between myself and tenant was a civil matter, and no business of the police. He then advised me that if I chose to do so, I could go to the local magistrate, and have a lien taken out on *all* of my

238

tenant's belongings at the house, until she paid the debt. If I was quick, I could have the order by this afternoon. At this piece of news, my tenant quickly agreed to leave the washing machine if I would let her take the rest of her things, with a promise to pay the balance 'as soon as possible'. We then had a long argument on the value of the washing machine, finally settled at RM600. All witnessed by the superintendent, who then departed.

Meanwhile Cheetah turned up. He was my long-time friend from down the road, who had just returned from Singapore, and heard I was back. He was in time to overhear the washing machine valuation, and offered to ask his sister to buy it. Apparently she was on the lookout for one right now, which proves the gods do occasionally smile. Cheetah told me he had a night shift job in Singapore, which would finish in another couple of days.

The truck returned half an hour late at 12.30, and we all pitched in with loading the furniture, minus washing machine. My ex-tenant was now all sweetness and light – butter wouldn't melt in her mouth even. I knew damned well I would never see the rest of my money as she waved goodbye. Cheetah's sister took the washing machine in return for cash payment, and Cheetah and I carried it along the street to their house. I now had some money in my pocket.

When I borrowed Cheetah's phone and plugged it into the outlet, the line had already been cut off. Telikom had waited until the bill reached the RM1,000 they owed me, then promptly cut the line.

Franky told me he had an Indonesian businessman friend who would like to rent the house, except for master bedroom and one bathroom/toilet; for the same as my ex-tenant had been paying for the whole house, if I paid the electricity and water bills. I said yes straight away.

CHAPTER 18

I spent the next few days sorting out the furniture, and cleaning up the garden. I pulled out a heap of overgrown weeds, and lightly forked over the area between the bushes. There was a sizeable clump of my original portulaca still lurking among the weeds, so I separated pieces and spaced them out. Then I pruned back my curry leaf bushes, bougainvillea and jasmine. The latter had become quite straggly over the front wall, the bougainvillea were threatening to take over most of the garden, and the curry leaf bushes were trying to be trees. Once pruned to my satisfaction I turned my attention to getting the Mini back on the road. Franky assured me his mechanic friend could fix the overheating problem very cheaply, so I gave him a go.

Meanwhile his business friend Musa and wife turned up, took one look at the house and agreed to my terms. They seemed quite a nice couple, who supplied Indonesian housemaids and factory workers to Johor Baru businesses. They had a small office about a kilometre from my house, where she spent most of her time. They were currently living with friends in rather cramped conditions, and were happy to move in straight away. There was just enough room in the carport for their Proton Saga car to park alongside the Mini, and still open the doors. With their rental payment and security deposit, plus the washing machine money, I was feeling quite flush. Before it could burn a hole in my pocket I paid the electricity bill, plus a 'special' road tax sticker for the Mini. Franky's mechanic fixed the overheating problem for RM50 – I wish I had met him earlier.

On my first Tuesday back in my own house I used Franky's mobile phone to call a plantation manager friend I had known well some years before in Perak. He was now managing an oil palm plantation less than an hour's drive away on the other side of Kota Tinggi. I told him we had Indonesian workers available, and he was immediately interested. He invited us to visit him tomorrow and have lunch with him. Twenty of Franky's men had recently arrived in JB, and were crowded into a couple of large rooms above a coffee shop near my new tenants' office.

We set off for Kota Tinggi in the Mini next morning with high hopes. At the other end we took a couple of wrong plantation roads before finding the one to Moktar's plantation, but were still early. Most important of all was that the Mini wasn't overheating. Moktar greeted us at the door of his large estate house, and within moments his houseboy produced a large jug of ice-cold lolly-water. My friend had prospered since I last saw him in Perak a few years ago. He was always tall for a Malaysian, and he now had an expensive-looking stomach to go with his height.

Lunch was a light affair of various snacks, ideal for the climate and time of day. Over it we discussed rates for the labourers. Moktar said he needed 12 right now, with maybe a few more later. He required the first lot for about 4 months. In the meantime he would put the word around his neighbours that we had labour available. In the end he agreed a rate 80% more

242

than Franky had set with the men. The estate would pay us the agreed rate, and we would then pay the lesser amount to the labourers. My half of the proceeds would cover at least my basic food costs for the next four months, and I had been back in JB for less than a week!

Back at the house Musa said he had applied for a new phone line in his name. We agreed to hook up my fax machine to the line, and I could put the number on the El Cheapo business cards Franky was getting made up for me. Incoming calls and faxes for me would be free in exchange for him using the fax machine. Suited me fine. Roughly translated my house address is 38 Lotus Street, Beautiful Johor Gardens, which will look good on the cards.

Thursday morning we collected 12 labourers from the coffee shop, and ferried them 4 at a time to the bus stop on the highway. Each was given bus fare, and the name of the stop at which they were to get off the bus. Their bedding and more bulky possessions were then loaded into the Mini van, and we drove to Moktar's plantation near Kota Tinggi. Having unloaded the belongings at the living quarters, we then picked up the men from the highway bus stop and ferried them to the plantation. The whole operation took less than two hours.

Moktar told us his neighbour needed the other eight men, plus four more as soon as possible. He took us to the neighbouring plantation and introduced us to the manager. We agreed to repeat today's operation tomorrow with the remaining eight men. We would make it early, because Friday is Moslem

Holy Day, and everyone disappears by lunchtime. Franky would then go to Batam for another four on Monday. Moktar told me on the way back to his place that he would require another 10 men in about 3 weeks time.

On Saturday I told Franky I would like to go to Batam with him on Monday, and kill two birds with one stone. I could look around at the operation and renew my Malaysian visa. I am supposed to stay out for at least a week this time, so I proposed to carry on to Karimun Island and look up some old friends from my time in jail there (*Tropical Trial*). I calculated that I had just enough spare money to pay a medium-cost Indonesian hotel for a week, plus expenses. It would be a great deal cheaper than trying to stay in Singapore for a week. I would also keep Moktar's requirement for ten more labourers in the back of my mind.

On Monday morning Franky's friend drove us to Pasir Gudang in his car. I had been in JB for quite some time, without knowing there was an Immigration gateway at Pasir Gudang, which means Warehouse Sands. From here many small ferries ply to Singapore and different Indonesian islands. There were about a dozen boats of various sizes at the piers when we arrived. We bought our tickets for Batam Island before passing quickly through Immigration.

Our boat had space for about 30 passengers, and we were on our way within half an hour of arriving. The boat was diesel powered, and built for sea-keeping rather than speed. I estimated our speed at about 12 knots. Franky said the trip

244

would take just under two hours, which made my speed estimate about right. The big fast boats from Singapore do the shorter crossing in about half an hour. But a ticket on one of them costs twice as much. Plus transport across Singapore, passing through Immigration three times. This little boat was already saving me a fair bit of money.

We arrived at the Batam pier about 10am. As we tied up I noticed *Maju Express* tied up 50 yards away, outside the Immigration/Customs area. The Immigration man asked the purpose of my visit, and like an idiot I said business.

"Ah," says he, "A business visa will cost Rp50,000, tourist visa only Rp20,000."

I looked him straight in the eye, then said in my best Indonesian

"Hey, I'm not a rich American tourist, your visa too expensive."

"Ah, you speak Indonesian very well. For you tourist visa only Rp10,000, thankyou."

Franky gave me a big grin as we left the building, and told me I sure know how to deal with his countrymen. I asked him to accompany me to *Maju Express* before going anywhere else. Captain Udin was on the pier near the boat, and saw us coming. He walked towards us with hand outstretched. "Mr Anderson, has been long time, welcome back to Indonesia."

He invited us on board for a cup of tea and chat. I told him I was planning to visit Karimun, and he insisted I travel with him for 'special price.' Tomorrow he is doing a shuttle service

245

back and forward to Singapore, but Wednesday he will be making a return trip to Karimun, leaving 10am, would that suit? I said it would suit very well thanks. He has recently spent a lot of money on a refit for the boat. She is a converted motor torpedo boat, and I know from experience that she can run like the wind. I've wondered a few times in the past if he ever indulges in a bit of smuggling, but it's impolite to ask!

After saying goodbye to Captain Udin we made our way to the carpark, where Franky negotiated a deal with a couple of tough-looking motorbike taxi drivers. The upshot was that they will remain with us for the next 48 hours, as drivers and bodyguards, for the princely sum of RM15 each plus petrol and food. They wear light jeans and denim shirts, with red bandanas on their heads – and sheathed knives at their waists. One has a scar on the left side of his face, while the other has a patch over his left eye. Presumably their opponents were both right-handed! They scare me, so I suppose they might scare any would-be pickpockets and such-like. Some areas of Batam are notorious for their pickpockets and opportunist robbers.

We traveled to our hotel on the pillion seats. I held on tight to my driver, who seems to fancy himself as a prospective motorcycle grand prix competitor. The hotel Franky picked was quite a pleasant surprise. It obviously hasn't been there long – the dwarf wall and garden in front not yet finished – and everything is new and clean. Unfortunately a few things don't quite work properly yet, but nothing very important.

We booked in and paid a night's accommodation in

advance. As soon as I had my 2 spare shirts on the hangers I suggested to Franky that we have lunch somewhere. He said hang on a little longer and we'll have lunch at the 'staging house'. Off we went once more on the great motorcycle race, dodging in among cars, buses and becas.

The staging house was quite a large highset colonial style house, biggest in the unpaved street. The effect had been somewhat spoiled by the fact that underneath the house had been turned into something akin to a rabbit warren. It was stuffed full of small rooms and narrow passageways. Franky was proud to show me his renovations, while I thought there was damned little to be proud of. This is where the labourers from other parts of Indonesia overnight for 'processing' on their way to Malaysia. It must be a lean time, because there were only a few people there.

Upstairs was a different matter, with large airy rooms. The lady who runs the house busied herself preparing lunch for us, after introducing me to her five daughters. Three of the daughters assisted Mum, while the two older ones, in their twenties, fussed over me. They fetched me the mandatory glass of tea, during the course of which the one with the shorter hair managed to brush against me. The other sister shot her a warning look, and I realized that they thought the orang puteh might make a good catch. I grinned at Franky, and prepared to 'endure' their attentions. Later I would ask Franky to tell them I am married, but now would be inconvenient for some reason.

Just as we finished lunch, a distinguished-looking

gentleman appeared. From the way everyone fawned over him I gathered he was someone of importance, even before being introduced. He was probably in his early sixties, nearly six feet tall, and looked in good trim. His name is Haji Hasbullah, and he is a local businessman. In conversation with him I mentioned that I had known a Mr Hasbullah in Palembang 25 years ago. He was then Deputy Chief of the Provincial Dept of Works. Haji declared what a small world it is, that was his elder brother. He became Chief of the Department for some years, and retired to the family home in Medan ten years ago. Last year he died from a heart attack. I expressed my condolences, accepted by Haji, who then wanted to know all about my time in Palembang. We talked in our own little world for more than half an hour.

At the end of it, Haji said I must spend tomorrow night at his large house as his guest. I glanced at Franky, who gave an almost imperceptible nod. We had provisionally arranged to spend tomorrow night at the staging house, because the hotel is rather pricy. We should have stayed at the staging house in the first place, but Franky had been too embarrassed to ask the white man to sleep there. The white man wouldn't have objected at all, he's used to all sorts of places. But with Indonesians you must always be on the outlook for them thinking they might lose face. I had been too preoccupied to think about it earlier – until I saw the hotel tariff.

In mid-afternoon we set off on a motorcycle tour of the northern part of Batam Island. Many Singapore companies are building factories and warehouses here as an overspill to their own crowded island. I'm sure the much cheaper labour available is also a large incentive. Franky told me this was a problem, as many of his labourers 'deserted' after he had paid their fares to get here from other parts of the country. As well as the new factories there are golf courses being set out, and a large marina. There are also some fancy houses being built for the Singapore management personnel.

That evening we went to the night market in town, where I managed to buy some kretek (clove) cigarettes of a brand I haven't seen before. They are just as good as Gudang Garam, and considerably cheaper. There were crowds of people at the market, pushing and jostling – a pickpocket's paradise. Our two bodyguards were kept busy making way for us, and glaring at any possible troublemakers. By 8pm we were seated in a Chinese restaurant with roof but no walls. Franky said they don't need walls because they never close!

Young ladies of the night kept trying to join us at our table, but I told Franky I'm not interested. So then the beautiful poondangs (boygirls) sensed an opportunity and moved in. I said I'm not interested in *them* either, and the bodyguards shooed them away. In the end we enjoyed a cheap and remarkably good meal, washed down with Bintang beer. We arrived back at the hotel not long after 11pm, much to Franky's disappointment. I think he fancied a night on the town with the girls, but I wanted a decent night's sleep. Let him creep around tomorrow night when I'm at Haji's house.

In the morning I moved my bag to Haji Hasbullah's

house, and spent most of the day there, while Franky wandered off. He was probably quite relieved to be on his own, and not responsible for me for a while. This suited me fine, as I just wanted to enjoy a relaxing day. Haji's house is a stately two-storey affair, with many rooms and servants' quarters. I was shown to a large upstairs bedroom with a high ceiling. It contained a comfortable double bed, beautiful loose carpets on the floor, and Indonesian landscape paintings on the walls. Haji wanted to put his BMW car at my disposal – he also had a large Mercedes - but I declined the offer with regret. I explained to him the deal we had made with the bikies, and that I didn't want to renege on it.

"Is that all that is worrying you, you are much too kind-hearted. Give your motorcycle man the money due to him, and I will get the servants to make up a food package for him. He will be more than happy with that, and I have plenty of people to look after you. That way everyone will be properly served, and no face lost." I agreed, having suddenly realized I had nearly caused *him* to lose face by refusing the BMW. There were two more classic cars in a garage at the rear of the house. One was a navy blue Mark V11 Jaguar in immaculate condition. The other nearly took my breath away. It was a fawn and gold Armstrong Siddeley Sapphire, a car I had fallen in love with in my early twenties. Haji had impeccable taste in motor cars.

Haji had a couple of business clients to attend to, so I spent the afternoon circumnavigating the island at the wheel of the BMW. For company I had two of Haji's servants, who might have looked more at home on World Champion Wrestling. There was a great amount of new building taking place almost everywhere I looked. For a while I truly regretted not taking up Colonel Abihasaan's offer to act as one of his construction 'advisers' when he was appointed Chairman of the Batam Island Development Authority – but that's another story.

In the evening, Haji and I spent a long time talking, over drinks and snacks. We covered a multitude of topics, and I felt he was sounding me out for something. More than twice he mentioned 'friends' of his in an unusual part the labour business. It gradually dawned on me that he was talking about smuggling people into Australia, in a most circumspect and cautious manner. In just as circumspect a manner I managed to get the message over that I would not be interested in such a thing.

We then discussed the Colonel, who had retired as Chairman of the Authority as a rich man in 1984. He is now quite an important noise in political circles in Jakarta, good luck to him. If I'd known that in 1985, I might have got a message to him from that jail on Karimun! I'm quite sure he would have done his best to help me – he got the Batam job on the back of my performance in Palembang. He knew it, and even sent me Christmas cards for a few years. I was late to bed, and late, for me, back out of it in the morning.

CHAPTER 19

Wednesday morning Haji's driver took me to the staging house, where I met up with Franky. The four additional labourers were ready to go, and I accompanied them and Franky to the ferry terminal. Their boat to Singapore was leaving half an hour before *Maju Express,* and I waved goodbye before crossing to the other pier to say hello to Captain Udin.

We cast off bang on time at precisely 10am, which is most unusual in Indonesia. *Maju Express* is renowned not only for its speed, but also punctuality. I spent more than half of the exhilarating journey on the 'bridge' with the captain. At one stage he pointed proudly at the speed gauge, which was just touching 40 knots. She must be guzzling fuel was my thought. But she carries 50 passengers in comfort, and is always well patronized. In spite of the fare being more than twice that of the slow boats. She is probably the fastest boat of her size in the region, and Captain Udin is justly proud of her, and his own reputation. It is a point of honour with him to always be on, or ahead of, time. This is doubly unusual in an area where timekeeping is generally lax.

I hardly recognized the waterfront at Karimun when we arrived. Gone was the old rickety pier of my first visit. In its place there were two new piers, with floating platforms alongside. Instead of a risky climb up a none-too-safe ladder at low tide, even old ladies can now safely step ashore onto these platforms. Then walk up the ramps joining them to the pier –

they even have wheels underneath, so they become steeper at low tide, and flatter at high tide!

At the shore end of the piers is a brand new hotel, where the old market used to be. I decided to walk to the Wisma Gloria hotel, and take in the new sights on the way. The waterfront was completely changed, but as I got closer to the hotel, the familiar houses were still there on each side of the street, between hotel and police station. The latter hasn't changed either, but somebody has given it a new coat of paint recently.

At the hotel I was met by the owner, who told me his wife was sick, but would be glad to see me later. I had known her as a busy robust person, while he, on the other hand, always seemed on the point of dying. He had been invalided out of the Indonesian navy with very bad lungs. His breathing is a continuous wheeze, but seems no worse than it was eleven years ago. In fact he looked almost the same as he had when I last saw him. On the other hand, I was devastated when I saw his wife later. She looks twenty years older, and a mere shadow of her former self. But still she managed a cheerful smile, and made me most welcome.

There was one obvious omission in the foyer, which was the large-scale model of the corvette on which the owner had served in the navy. I remarked on the fact, and asked where is it. He merely shrugged and said 'not here just now'. I didn't push, as he obviously didn't want to discuss the subject. I told them I would be staying for two nights, and they charged me share-a-room price. This worried me slightly, until I saw the room. It was a large four-bed room overlooking the water, but with only one bed made up – they had given me the room to myself at share price.

After a light lunch I went for a stroll to the jail, and had my next surprise. It was abandoned and empty. I even managed to walk straight in through the front door, through the guardroom entry, and into the small compound. There wasn't a soul in sight, and everything was just rotting away – everything that wasn't already rotten that is. Cell doors were off their hinges, the compound gate was lying on the ground, and half the fence was missing. It is obviously no longer an active jail.

I went back outside and stood in the road contemplating the desolation. No regrets mind you, because the place wasn't fit for human habitation when it *was* in service, never mind now. I waved a passing motorcyclist to a stop, and asked him what had happened to the jail. He told me it has been closed for more than a year, and everyone has been moved to the big new jail outside the town. When I asked him how could I get there, he said no problem, he could take me. His house is near the jail, and he is going home soon anyway, just a couple of errands to do first – hop on!

It took him only ten minutes to complete his errands before we headed out of town, via the 'high' road. As I dismounted outside the big new jail, there was a cry from within

"Mister Anderson, Mister Anderson" Out stepped King Kong, the big guard I had christened with that name – I had given them all nicknames. I discovered later that he was still known by my nickname, and quite proud of it. He called my name another couple of times while shaking hands and giving me a bearhug. Smiley and The Milky Bar Kid came running to extend their greetings, the latter no longer a 'kid'. A table and chairs appeared in the open area outside the guardroom, while tea was ordered for the guest of honour. I felt like the returned Prodigal.

We chatted for nearly an hour. I asked about the prisoners' conditions, and was told the guards now received better pay than before. They have their own small farm for growing staple food, so they no longer have to steal the prisoners' food. There is a larger farm for the inmates, worked by trusties. Finally they now have a quartermaster whose job is to see that the prisoners have enogh food at all times. Changed days indeed. No more inmates unable to walk because of vitamin A deficiency. In fact the inmates I could see through the chainlink fence looked much healthier than in my day. The open compound is very large, with a soccer field and volleyball area.

The jail now holds about twice as many as the old one, but with something like five times the living area. I was disappointed not to meet Abdul Gani, the Deputy Commandant of the old jail. But happy for him, as he has been promoted to Cmmandant of the large jail in Tanjungpinang, The Provincial capital. I'm quite sure the prisoners in that jail will have benefited from having him as Cammandant.

I'd been a little worried about how to get back to town, but my 'taxi' driver was invited to join us at the table, as he knew some of the guards. They in turn informed him what a great guy I am, helping Indonesian prisoners even when I was unwell myself, defying the old Commandant and police chief, blah, blah, blah. He seemed impressed by their exaggerations, then pricked up his ears when I told the guards I was finding work on Malaysian plantations for a few Indonesian labourers. His name is Yusup Harkono, and when it was time to leave, he asked me to his house for further conversation. "Don't worry, I take you back to town after."

The house is a well-ventilated lowest 3-bedroom affair. Nothing fancy, but the basics are all there, including electricity and water. His wife is charming, and made me a cool lollywater pink drink in a tall glass. It turns out that Yusup is some kind of local youth social worker, or that's how he put it. He explained that although Karimun is booming, most of the jobs require education and/or experience. Which leaves out many of the local youths – could I help? If we pay transport and visa costs, they will work for a very low rate, provided accommodation and food supplied in Malaysia.

I did a quick calculation and realized they would be cheaper than the others, provided the extra under-table payments for documents were not exorbitant. Yusup informed me there is a direct ferry service from Karimun straight to Kukup in Malaysia, much shorter than going via Batam. From Kukup there are plenty of buses to JB. He produced an atlas and showed me where Kukup is. Just a stonesthrow from Karimun! The direct service goes twice a week, and takes only an hour and a half.

Yusup gave me a lift into the Immigration office before going about his own business. I asked to see the Immigration Chief, but was fobbed off at first. As I sat in the outer office wondering what to do next, a middle-aged Immigration officer walked over to me with his hand extended.

"Mister Anderson hello, I'm Alwi, do you remember me?"

"Oh, yes, Mr Alwi, how are you?"

I didn't remember him, but didn't want to tell him that. Then I vaguely recalled his face as one of the ones who stopped Liz and me from catching the fast boat on my second last day on the island back in 1985. So I took a punt, with fingers crossed.

"You were the walkie-talkie radio man, right?"

He beamed at me and puffed out his chest.

"Yes, yes, that was me, you do remember."

I told him I had come to see the Chief, but nobody seemed interested. He filled me in on the current situation. Mr Sutadji, the old Chief, is now in Jakarta following promotion. His former Deputy Chief was also promoted and posted out. There is now a new Chief Mr Kunawan, posted in from Bali.

"Don't worry Mister Anderson, he is a good man. I will go now and tell him about you, and I am sure he will see you."

Ten minutes later, up strode a man in his late forties, very neatly dressed in uniform.

"Good afternoon Mister Anderson, Alwi has been telling me about you. I am Kunawan the new Chief of Immigration, how can I help you? Let us go next door and talk there, it's more comfortable. Another of my officers also remembers you and can join us."

We chatted in the beer garden of the new hotel, where they 'persuaded' me to have a couple of bottles of Bintang Baru – brown bottles, not green thanks. When I mentioned the plantation labourers, Mr Kunawan was very keen. He said the authorities are worried about local unemployed youths making trouble, and any I could find work for in Malaysia would be well out of it. Therefore he is prepared to expedite the necessary documents at the base price, and would accept no 'coffee money'.

The more I delved into this ex-Karimun labour proposition, the more attractive it was looking. No doubt Yusup would collect something from the families of the youths, but that was not really my concern. Nevertheless I made a mental note to ask him to demand only the necessary minimum for him to retain face and standing.

I arrived back at the Wisma Gloria just in time for a late snack of half a dozen chicken satay sticks from the hawker at the front gate. At the rate I was going, my expenditure would be considerably less than I had originally estimated. Yusup has suggested I go back to Malaysia the short way via Kukup. I think that's a good idea, as I want to check out the route myself anyway. Always better to check for yourself whenever possible. Problem is the boat makes the trip on Monday and Thursday, and tomorrow is Thursday. Besides which I already made provisional arrangements with people to travel back to Batam on Friday.

It was raining in the morning, and Yusup picked me up in a small Toyota car he had borrowed from a friend. We drove to a Malay shop for roti prata. He also solved my problem.His Chinese friend runs a computer shop, and is happy to act as our contact. Yusup has no phone at the house, and we will need to communicate. Would I like to meet Mr Lim, and call Batam to let them know my change of plan? Friday I can move into Yusup's spare bedroom until the boat leaves on Monday.

We finished breakfast and drove to the computer shop. Lim is a small chubby man with a cheerful smile, behind spectacle lenses that look like they belong in the bottom of a bottle. He ushered us into his private office, past the three employees working in the outer office. More tea was sent for, and I proceeded to drink my fifth glass of the morning. I was always a tea Jenny, so I managed to put it to bed quite comfortably. But I did decline the offer of a second glass – even we tea Jennies have our limits. Besides which, they always tend to make the tea too sweet for my taste. Mr Lim's tea comes in a tall glass with plastic lid, and contains at least twice as much as a normal teacup.

I paid Mr Lim for my calls to Haji Hasbullah in Batam and franky in JB. Franky was happy to hear I could source the required ten labourers from Karimun, as his further supplies are 'unavailable for now', whatever that means. So much for all his talk about having three hundred labourers ready to go to

Malaysia. I already started wondering about that when I saw the staging house nearly wmpty. But most Malays are prone to overstatement that way.

The next few days were busy for me. After moving my bag – I always travel with only one – to Yusup's house, we managed to achieve a great deal. I insisted on meeting all of the young men selected by Yusup for work in Malaysia. Mainly because I wanted to make sure Yusup wasn't doing a Franky on me, but I also wanted to look them over. They were a good looking bunch, and I chatted to most of them. Some were shy to talk at first, but I managed to get most of them to relax. I decided they are better overall than the ones Franky is supplying. Most of them are young, fit and polite, with no blowhards among them likely to cause trouble. There is one natural leader among them, in his early thirties. I might just pay him a little extra, to keep them on the straight and narrow.

Next on the agenda was Mr Kunawan at Immigration, who promised to have all the documentation ready for them to leave in less than three weeks. This would allow a week's leeway for any hitches. I paid him for this in advance, and still had enough cash to last until I get home. To make sure of that, I had first gone to the ferry office to book, and pay for, my ticket to Kukup on Monday.

Altogether there were nearly a hundred labourers willing to work in Malaysia, but I warned Yusup I could not guarantee anything beyond the first ten at this stage. But I did undertake to try and find work for as many as possible. Quite a few people from Karimun are already working in Malaysia, but most of them have arranged things themselves, or through relatives. There is no organized labour pipeline to Malaysia as such, so I have come to the right place at the right time. The labour agents that do exist on Karimun are all concentrating on placing skilled labour on the island from surrounding areas of the country. Most of the unskilled labour on the island has already been absorbed by the construction boom. 'My' lot are rural people who simply don't want to work on construction sites in town. They want to work on plantations.

At 4pm (5pm Malaysian time) on Monday I waved goodbye to my new friends as the ferry sailed for Kukup. By the time I got ashore, dusk was fast approaching. The ferry terminal is at the end of a narrow isthmus, down which runs a sealed road, with shops and houses on each side. I ducked into a restaurant for a snack, and to ask directions to the JB buses. Kukup Is a busy little place, being the Immigration entry point for people from all over the Riau Province of Indonesia, and the western half of the Riau Archipelago. The bus station was another 300 yards or so, where the small peninsula widens out. There are buses to Melaka and Keluang, as well as Johor Baru.

I squeezed on board a JB bus as it was about to leave. The driver said "No, no, full already." I told him never mind, I'll stand. For all I knew this might be the last bus of the day to JB, and it was already after dark. The driver's offsider shrugged and took my fare. He didn't give me a ticket, so I probably just made them their bonus for the trip. Most bus drivers in Malaysia are speed merchants, and this one was no exception. I put my bag between my feet, held onto the luggage rack, and kept my knees bent for the next hour, until the bus stopped at Skudai. Five passengers got off here and three got on, so I had a seat for the rest of the trip.

I arrived at JB new bus station just before 9pm, rather tired. There are no direct buses to Taman Johor Jaya from the new station, and I wasn't looking forward to catching one bus into the city and another back out again. This trip is rather like an elongated V, when all I needed to do was cross the top of the V. Unfortunately, with paying documentation and so on, I had cut the money situation very fine – not quite enough left for a taxi. But there was a very pleasant surprise awaiting me. Franky met me off the bus, and drove me home in the mini van. We were home in twenty minutes, instead of the hour plus it would have taken by bus. My main worry now was that Kukup Immigration had given me only a two-week visa.

Over the next fortnight I visited our labourers and their bosses three times a week, to make sure there were no problems. I liked to visit a little before lunchtime, so there was time for the bosses to have my lunch prepared! It was usually delicious – and free. What with three free lunches a week, and the income from the labourers, I am starting to make ends meet, for the first time this year. Then it was visa renewal time again.

I decided to make a quick trip across the Causeway to Singapore and back. Unfortunately the Gods were in particularly frivolous mood on the day I chose. I passed through Malaysian

Immigration before remembering that I can no longer just hop on board a Singapore 120 bus at the Causeway. Now that the new JB bus station is in service, you have to go all the way out there if you want to cross by bus. I decided to walk across to Singapore, since it's less than a mile. But by then it was fairly pouring rain, and guess who didn't bring his umbrella? I stood under the canopy in No-Man's-Land waiting for the rain to stop; and waiting for the rain to stop….and waiting….

After about an hour of bucketing rain I decided it didn't want to stop at all, so I hatched a little plan. I walked along the fence dividing incoming Immigration from outgoing Immigration. Round the end of the fence, and back along again. Now I was on the incoming side, so I confidently presented my passport at one of the booths. The Indian Immigration man got halfway through his welcome to Malaysia spiel, before pausing with a puzzled look on his face.

"Sir, you are having a Malaysian exit stamp, but where is your Singapore chop?"

I started to tell him about the heavy rain, no umbrella……

"But that is not being allowed sir, it is illegal. You must be coming with me to see my superior officer. You are being in very big trouble sir."

I was hustled to the back of the booth, then up a flight of stairs to the offices of The Almighty. The God upstairs was a Malay, so I told him my funny little story in Bahasa. He grinned before becoming more serious.

"You must understand that this is against the rules Mr

Anderson, but I can understand your concern. It is very heavy rain, and you were not to know the Singapore bus service has been changed. Therefore, since you also have had the courtesy to learn the Malay language, I will overlook it just this once. I will even help you to solve the problem, if you will follow me."

He headed out the door with my passport in his hand, Anderson hot on his heels. We went to a gate in the dividing fence, which he opened with a key. We were now back on the departures side, and we walked across to the far side of the road. For a few minutes we just stood there, until a Singapore 120 bus appeared. My benefactor stepped onto the road and held up his hand for the bus to stop.

"Take this man across the Causeway please," says he to the driver. "Here's your passport Mr Anderson, and please don't do it again."

The passengers on the bus stared at me as I sat down near the driver. They were probably wondering what small crime I had committed in order to be deported by bus! The driver didn't ask me for the fare, so it was a free trip as well as a dry one. The bus dropped us all at the Singapore Immigration hall, and I headed for the almost deserted lane marked 'Other Commonwealth Countries.' The Immigration lady scanned her computer, but I wasn't on today's list of wanted criminals, so she stamped my passport and welcomed me to Singapore. She didn't forget to add 'again.'

CHAPTER 20

Two weeks later ten labourers arrived from Karimun for Mr Makmur, in two batches of five each. Franky picked them up in the mini van and drove them straight to the plantation. One in the front passenger seat, four in the back, plus belongings, filled the van to capacity. That little van is now earning its keep, and I'm glad I hung onto it. Makmur and his neighbour let me know they will be standing down the labourers for about ten weeks, from before Christmas until after Hari Raya. This gives me less than three months to find alternative gainful employment for them and myself.

Meanwhile I faxed Singapore a couple of weeks ago, confirming my approval for Liz to fly home when it can be safely arranged. More than that I cannot easily do, since her family in Singapore are being very uncooperative. The only one I can get any information from is Uncle Buang, the black sheep of the family in JB. But they are starting to keep him in the dark also, knowing he passes information on to me. While in jail I thought how good they were to help us out, but I was soon disillusioned after my release. Patrick presented me with a bill for everything they had done for me and Liz. Including taking care of Grace while Liz and Gina were in Australia.

An explanation might be a good idea at this stage. Grace is the illegitimate daughter of my wife's sister Lydia, who is also the sister of Patrick's wife Shirley. Lydia is the naughty girl of the family, having had two previous illegitimate children; one of

265

whom was adopted by Patrick and Shirley. When Liz and I heard that Lydia was pregnant once more, we decided to adopt the child when it was born, boy or girl. During the pregnancy I paid all medical costs, and supported Lydia with food and money. I then paid the hospital bills. When Grace was 36hrs old, I took her home with me from the hospital.

Patrick registered the birth, with my name entered as the father. I found out later that in fact, he registered the real father, not me. I think now that he had a future option in mind even then. For nearly eight years Liz and I took very good care of Grace, giving her all the love and affection a child should have.

In Sitiawan Perak, we had an Indian Tamil amah, and many Chinese friends. Grace grew up learning not only English, but Hokien and Tamil also. When she was a baby I carried her in a large sling, reminiscent of a broken arm. When she began to walk, I would take her with me in the car to different plantations where I had people working. Whenever we had the chance I would take her into the rubber plantation near the house, on Gina's bike. This was a small mountain bike, so I had to splay my legs while pedaling, so my knees wouldn't hit the handlebars. I would crouch forward on the bike, with Grace on my back, arms round my neck. Of we would go along the pathways, looking for monkeys, butterflies, flowers and frogs.

On one occasion while still quite small, she tugged at my trousers, calling

"Daddy, Daddy, kokolat."

"No, you've had enough chocolate for today, no more

until tomorrow."

But she kept repeating it, while tugging on my trousers and pointing to the carport. So I let her tow me outside, where she promptly pointed out a frog. She hadn't been asking for chocolate at all, she was saying the Tamil word for frog!

For years she was my special little girl. When Liz went to America two years ago, Patrick and Shirley put their plan into effect. Shirley can't conceive a child of her own, which is why they adopted previously. They literally stole Grace from me while in Singapore, with the full backing of the law.. I was also banned from contacting Grace for a minimum of two years, so that 'her emotions can be fully transferred to her new adoptive parents.' I have in fact twice secretly met her at McDonalds in Singapore without Patrick's knowledge. If caught I would probably be put in jail, but Grace won't tell. She is part of the reason I have hung around here, but I may not be able to do so much longer if I can't sell any of my writing.

I have started answering advertisements in the newspapers for construction jobs in Malaysia and Singapore. Not a great deal of hope right now, unless some company is desperate for someone of my experience. They would have to get a Work Permit for me; so it is easier for them to employ a local, or someone who already has a Work Permit that can be transferred.

I would contact AGK Pacific in Papua New Guinea, but that wouldn't do much good. I quit them partly because I considered the company was being mismanaged after the owner had a stroke. The two men jointly running it were like chalk and cheese, so if one said yes, the other automatically said no. Each sat in his own office, and was most unwilling to talk to the other. They held diametrically opposed views on how the company should be run, and there was no third party with the authority to break the stalemate. You simply cannot run a successful company that way. Since then they have been gradually selling off assets and sinking lower, which is a shame, as it was a very good company. One of them has now left the company, and the other occasionally sends me a fax with the gory details. He's still hoping for the 'big one' for which he will want me back, but I'm not counting on it any time soon.

Meanwhile I'm keeping up my visits to the plantations, to the point where the bosses reckon my 'after sales service' is the best in the business! They have put the word around about me, but nobody wants to take on more labour too close to the slack period – it would take me a minimum of three weeks to get more here from Karimun. In February, after Hari Raya, there will probably be a big demand, but that's a long time to keep the belt tightened. My half of the income from the labourers is just enough to cover my personal use of phone and fax, computer software and paper, half the business cost and all my private cost of the Mini van, and a few beers now and again. The rent covers basic things like food and smokes, plus visa renewal trips and a little in reserve for possible interviews.

A couple of weeks before Christmas the owner of the Blue Room phoned and asked me to call in to his office some time soon. The Blue Room is where I go at least once a week for the best fish and chips in Malaysia, accompanied by a Heineken beer. The Chinese owner has his office upstairs, where he deals in plumbing and small construction projects. When I visited his office nhe said he was planning to expand in the construction business, would I be interested? I told him I'm definitely interested, what does he have in mind?

Tenders are about to be called for a large new housing estate to the east of Taman johor jaya. It will comprise 400 houses and 80 shophouses, complete with necessary roadworks, drainage, sewerage etc. He will have the tender documents in early January, with tenders closing end of February. He would like me to work with him on making up the tender. He offered me RM1,000 to help him make up the tender, which I accepted.

I know it's no use ringing Patrick for information on Liz, and Uncle Buang is now being told nothing. So I've rung the other sister in Singapore several times. Each time I get 'The number you are calling is no longer in service.' Directory Enquiries say there is no new number for that name. That sounds peculiar to me, because her husband needs the phone. But most of his calls are outgoing – maybe he now has a silent number? In which case Enquiries won't give it out. Next visa trip I'll go and knock on some Singapore doors.

On 21st December I got Franky to drive me to the main bus station. The old bus station is now closed, and Zainal has opened an office at the new one. He must have made some arrangement with his creditors. Before I left Kelantan he was scared to come back to JB. Maybe I'll get some of my money back after all, and maybe not. I showed my face at his office so he knows I'm still around, before catching the Singapore bus.

SBS run a shuttle service from the new bus station to Queen Street in Singapore, so whatever time you arrive, there will be a bus soon. They run nearly full most of the day, with sometimes a long wait to squeeze on one at rush time.. So I tend to use them in mid-morning, early afternoon or late evening. At the Causeway the bus drops you at the entry side of the Immigration hall, then drives through to pick up waiting passengers at the exit side. The process is repeated at the Singapore end. Unless you are *very* quick through Immigration, you end up doing the trip in three different buses – so don't lose your original ticket. Many of the Mercedes, MAN and Volvo buses have bodies supplied by Alexander in Scotland. The bus boides are white, with ALEXANDER on the rear, in blue capital letters. Except for the 'X', which is white on a blue square, denoting the flag of Scotland – neat!

I caught the MRT train from Queen Sreet to Bedok, where the other sister lives. It's about a half mile walk from the station to the flat, which is on the sixth floor of a large block. I stopped for a couple of curry puffs and tea at the coffee shop in the ground floor, since I hadn't yet eaten breakfast, and it was nearly 11am. When I knocked on the door of the flat, there was a quick movement at the window curtain, followed by silence. I knocked again without response. After the fourth knock it was obvious whoever was inside didn't want to talk to me, so I left. But I only went as far as the coffee shop, where I dallied over another curry puff and tea. Maybe I could catch them by surprise, so I gave it half an hour before taking the elevator to the sixth floor once more. Eithet r they were expecting me back, or I had imagined the movement at the curtain, because the result was the same. I was sure there was somebody at home. Quite apart from the curtain movement, I know she goes out to work, while he stays home with their handicapped daughter.. After the fifth knock I gave up and went back to the MRT station, where I caught a train to Tampines. This is where Patrick lives. I didn't hold out much hope with him, but I had to at least try.

His flat is more than a mile from the MRT station, so I caught the local bus from the bus exchange next to the station. Singapore public transport is very well organized. My first two knocks at Patrick's door were met by silence. At the third knock, Shirley's voice shouted

"Go away!"

I knocked again,a dn she shouted once more

"I don't want to talk to you."

"But I want to talk to you, and I want to know what's happening with my wife."

"You have to talk to Patrick about that, and he won't be back until tomorrow. Anyway, you're not supposed to come here. If you don't go away, I'll call the police."

She probably would too, and the Singapore neighbourhood Police are very quick to respond. I decided to

271

get out of there fast, just in case she called them anyway.The MRT train didn't take long back to Queen Street, where I boarded the 120 bus to JB. I walked out of Malaysian Immigration at 4pm, with a two-month visa! My Immigration friend from the walk-round-the-fence escapade had spotted me while doing his rounds. He told the Maly lady in the booth to give me two months "So he doesn't bother us so often", with a big grin on his face. Instead of re-boarding the 120 bus, I walked a few hundred yards along the street, and caught the Johor Bus Service bus straight to the stop 400 yards from my house. I interrupted my walk with a stop for murtabak and beer at my local coffee shop, and was still home in time to trim the curry leaf bush before dark.

Christmas was quite a lively affair, with little presents and cards from my local friends. I didn't realize until now just how many friends I have made in the neighbourhood. Cheetah and the two Romanian forklift salesmen from down the road treated me to dinner at the local fancy Chinese restaurant on Christmas Day. This was followed by free beers at the Blue House. Photos were taken of me with the waitresses beside the Blue House Christmas tree, and a good time was had by all. I even managed a few vigorous dances with the staff on the pocket-handkerchief dance floor. On Boxing Day I woke up with my first hangover in years.

In January I was busy with the Blue House tender. In the middle of the month I received a fax from Barry in PNG. He has submitted a tender for Busu Road in Lae, and looks like getting the contract, will I come as Project manager? I replied that I'd be delighted, then explained as tactfully as possible about the housing estate tender. Back came a fax stating he is sure of getting the contract, as AGK have already been recommended to AusAID as the best tenderer. But there is a problem with the signing of the contract, which might take a month or more. If he puts me on half salary now, will I promise to come as soon as it's signed? This contract has to be done right, and make a profit, and I'm the only one he can trust to accomplish that.

How could I refuse such an offer? I showed the fax to Mr Chan at the Blue House. He thought for a few moments before saying

"Go for it, we've got no guarantee of getting the housing contract. That fax proves you're the man to do it if I do get it, but it looks like this man really needs you. I'd tell him yes if I were you, and we'll just see what happens."

It looks like Christmas has come for me again very early.

On 28th January I went to the rasa Sayang Hotel to see Uncle Buang bin Hussein, to give him his full title. He is a real old rascal, but usually treats me well enough, in return for favours – usually money 'for the family'. As soon as he gets it he goes nightclubbing, and the family get what's left, but at least they get something! He had been about to come and see me with news of Liz, he said. The adults in Singapore still aren't confiding in him, but one of his friends with a soft spot for me gave him some important information. She is the neighbourhood gambling queen in her neck of the woods, and gets to know

273

most things. According to her, Liz arrived back in Singapore about three months ago, and is in KK Hospital. Singapore Airlines finally came to the party and flew her home free, still in coma. Hospital costs are being met from her CPF account – the one I put the money into so I couldn't spend it.

I gave Uncle Buang a hug and fifty Ringgit, and rushed home to the phone. But when I rang KK Hospital I met a blank wall. Sorry, there is nobody of that name in the hospital. I asked them to check under her maiden name, just in case, but that also drew a blank. I then rang most of the other hospitals – there are plenty of them in Singapore – but without success. I sat down and tried to figure out what the hell is going on. Why are her family deliberately keeping all of this from me? Is that why nobody will open the door and talk to me? What are they up to? What do they hope to gain from doing this? Nasty thoughts started flitting through my mind. I know to my cost that they are a mercenary lot. When I returned from jail on Karimun they already 'owned' all of my furniture, television, stereo and so on. Bought from Liz at ridiculously low prices 'to help her out.' The only valuable thing left was my collection of Bavarian crystal. My mother-in-law knew what they are like, and promised not to let any of them get their hands on it. She kept it all safely in her flat, where she could see it, because she really loved it. When she died – in my absence – it immediately disappeared. It took about eight years for me to collect it all, in matching pieces, and it was insured for A$16,000 when shipped from Australia to Singapore in 1984.

CHAPTER 21

For most of February I've been working on the Blue House tender. I set a pattern, working at Mr Chan's office on Monday, Wednesday and Saturday. Sometimes I take a problem back to the house, so I can put some extra thought into it. I've visited the site six times already, just to check on ground conditions, existing services and so on. Tuesday, Thursday and Sunday I visit the plantations and fly the flag. Most of the men seem happy to see me take such an inerest in them. There was one problem about the food being given to the men at Makmur's neighbouring plantation. I managed to sort it out amicably, before it escalated.

Both plantations had decided to hold onto our Indonesian labourers over the extended holiday period of Christmas, New Year, Hari Raya and Chinese New Year. This was because, although the amount of work to be done was less, the number of Malaysian workers available would be insufficient. A greater number of Malays than usual had opted to 'Balik kampong' (go back to home vollage) for the entire month of Puasa. I now manage a free lunch on most days of the week. The Blue House throws in lunch on the house on my days there, and Makmur would be offended if I didn't lunch with him at his place – or so I tell myself.

Today 26th February, I received a fax from Barry, saying the contract is signed, get moving. Perfect timing, as I finished the tidying up on the housing tender yesterday morning.

Included with the fax is a Letter of Appointment, and approval from Immigration for my position. Tomorrow I go to Kuala Lumpur by train, for my Work Permit and visa from the PNG High Commission.

KL's main railway station was busy when my overnight train arrived from JB in the early hours of the morning. The new Light Rail system has just started functioning, so I made enquiries to find out if it goes anywhere near the PNG Hicom. The wall map shows there is a station about half a mile from the Hicom, and the frist train leaves at 5.30am.

I walked around until I found the Hicom at 6.30am, just so I know where it is. Then I waited for half an hour outside the local classy-looking coffee shop before it opened. It is quite a pretentious place, calling itself the Euro Bistro. Imagine my surprise when I discovered they serve bacon and eggs for breakfast, complete with choice of juice, plus toasted rolls and marmalade. With my recent increase in income, and a job to go to, I felt justified in enjoying it all, and they even had Earl Grey tea! I lingered for a while over my Earl Grey, remembering my secretary in Brisbane. I once walked quietly through from my office into hers, just as she was asking a visitor if he would like 'some of the boss's poofter tea.' I was still much too early for the Diplomatic Corps, so I walked round the block a couple of times, before having a glass of teh tarik at a roadside stall. First thing I did when the Hicom doors opened was ask directions to the toilet.

It took them only an hour or so to confirm my approval

with Waigani, and by 10.30 I was on my way, complete with Work Permit and visa in my passport. Being accustomed to the time-wasting and downright laziness of their compatriots back home, I had been prepared to spend most of the day at the Hicom. Now what should I do? My train to JB was due to leave at 8pm, and I didn't want to waste most of the day in KL. I took the light railway back into town, then walked to the Interstate bus station. It's as quick to walk as take a taxi, and cheaper. The streets of KL are incredibly congested, and the bus station is just as bad. I threaded my way through throngs of people to a booth selling tickets to JB and Singapore, and I hit the jackpot. There was a VIP express bus leaving in half an hour. It would get me to the causeway well before the last bus left town for Taman Johor Jaya, and do so in comfort. The VIP express bus costs about a third more than the ordinary express bus, but has fewer seats – which recline – and more legroom. I was home in my own bedroom by 10pm, tired but happy.

I'm now looking forward to my return to PNG, so I can get back to what I'm good at. I've never been good at running my own business and getting rich on it. Yes, it happened once, but with a fair slice of luck. As a rich man for a while, I found out that when you are rich, you tend to spend money on a lot of things you don't need. I care too much for the people who work for me to put my personal aggrandizement ahead of their needs. In other words I don't have the necessary killer instinct to be a permanently successful businessman. The liquidator of my company in Brisbane said "My god Brai, this isn't a company,

277

it's a big family." I took that as a compliment, whatever way he may have meant it.

I had more than a hundred employees, and I knew and cared for every one of them, including their wives and children. The company had a thriving Social Club, in which I refused to hold office, but joined as an ordinary member. For ecery dollar the employees contributed, the company put in two dollars. We had a weekend 'do' at least once a month. Cricket (and beer) with Operators versus The Rest; boating and water skiing at the dam, cruises down the river, and frequent Dance Nights. The dances were very popular, as we didn't have to hire a band – we had our own very good Country & Western band. My senior supervisor played the fiddle like a professional; the truck foreman was a semi-professional Hawaii guitar player, with half a dozen men of various skills on acoustic and electric guitars. I even occasionally (after a few beers) contributed my own amateur services on my King clarinet. I once placed a famous advertisement in the Brisbane Courier Mail for a 50-ton reardump truck operator specifying 'preference will be given to applicants able to play the drums.'

This road I'm going to build is important to Lae. In 1992 I was Project manager on construction of the Lae Industrial Estate at Malahang, on the outskirts of the city. At the time, I told the local politicians and AusAID representative that there was no way businessmen were going to build or lease factories out there until they had a decent road linking it with the docks, including a new bridge over the Bumbu River. I reminded them again in late 1994, while PM on the IFC Fish Factory and canning plant next door to the industrial estate. The rich Malaysians who paid for the fish factory have more political clout than me. Now it's finally being done, with AGK constructing the road, and Downer Construction building the new bridge. I wanted to build that bridge, as it's a long time since I built one, but my time will probably come.

On Wednesday 1st March I went into the travel agents at the Holiday Inn, where I picked up my ticket to PNG. I'm booked to leave Singapore Friday evening, arriving in Port Moresby 6am local time. Two days to sort out my affairs here. While in town I went to see Uncle Buang, to tell him my news, and find out if he had any more news on Liz. His source in Singapore had heard some vague rumours that Liz is in a private nursing home, but no details. My heart sank, as there are literally hundreds of such places in Singapore, many of which are not even listed in the Yellow Pages. I decided that as soosn as I have enough money in the bank in PNG, I will hire a private detective to find out what is happening to my wife.

Thursday evening I had the sniffles, becoming worse on Friday. I went to the local pharmacy for some antibiotics, just in case. But, being run by Malays, it was closed for Moslem holy day. On the way back I called on my Chinese medicine shop friend Mr Lai. He has no antibiotics, but made up for me a Chinese herbal remedy he thinks will help. I enjoy watching him making up his medicines from various ingredients in large glass jars, on his hand-held scales. Since the cold wasn't too bad I didn't worry too much about it. On the bus to Singapore it started to get worse, so once I had booked in and received my boarding pass, I went in search of a pharmacy. Singapore Airport is like a small town, so I had no trouble in finding a pharmacy in the huge departure hall. Unfortunately they wouldn't sell me antibiotics without a prescription, and directed me to the airport clinic. The doctor was at the other terminal, but would be back in an hour. A fat lot of good that was to me, as boarding time was only twenty minutes away; and there was no way I was going to miss that flight. In Malaysia – and PNG – you can buy antibiotics at the pharmacy without a doctor's prescription. But in Singapore the doctors are much better organized – and richer.

While serving in the Army as a young man, I came very close to dying from double broncho-pneumonia. Ever since then I've had to be very careful whenever I catch a cold, as it's liable to go quickly into my chest and cause an infection. By the time supper was served on the plane I was feeling decidedly unwell, and knew I was starting to run a fever. I slept fitfully for the remainder of the flight, and had a bad headache on landing. There was less than half an hour between landing and the departure of my flight to Lae. Not for the first time, I was thankful for my habit of traveling with carry-on cabin baggage only. It was therefore head of the queue for me at Customs, after a short delay at the Immigration counter. Customs waved me through the Nothing to Declare lane with my bag and briefcase, and I ran to the domestic terminal. They were calling my name as I arrived, so I went straight to the departure door, where they gave me a boarding pass. Ten minutes later I was airborne on my way to Lae, with an increasing headache and temperature.

My condition was not helped by the fact that the PNG gentleman next to me hadn't bathed for a while. His body odour was overpowering, and as soon as the seat belt sign went off, I hurried to the toilet and vomited in the bowl. I splashed my hot face with water, and more water, and stayed in the toilet until somebody banged on the door. I then stood in the aisle outside, until a hostess came and asked if anything was wrong. I explained my condition as well as I could, and she called the chief hostie. This magnificent lady 'just happened' to have some antibiotics in her bag, and didn't require a doctor's prescription. She gave me a couple of capsules, and a container of orange juice to wash them down. I have seldom been so grateful to a stranger. Thank God it's only a 35-minute flight, and I was soon in a company vehicle on the long trip into town from Lae Nadzab Airport. That journey takes as long as the flight from Moresby, so I offered up thanks once more to my Florence Nightingale of the skies. I bought more antibiotics as soon as the pharmacies opened.

Barry had several rental houses for me to look at in town, as they had sold the company house I lived in previously, along with most of the others, except the one he lives in himself. But I told him I wanted a house as near as possible to the job site. That way we could also use it as site office, which he didn't otherwise have available. Straight away he said Hilmer Wong

281

has built some houses at the Chinatown end of the new road, and a couple are available for rent. He'd thought I might not like to live in Chinatown, and so close to the Gun Club. We drove to Hilmer's new houses, which are in a compound of their own, with security at the gate. I took a quick look at a 2-storey furnished duplex, said okay, and the lease agreement was signed. No need for hotel bills, I'll move in tonight.

I spent Sunday in the house, going over the drawings and contract documents for the project. Barry had a spare sloping drawings table at the office, which we transported and set up in the large lounge of the house. At one end it had a rack for suspending large drawings, so I was set up already. By evening I was familiar with the basic design and specifications, and my headache was subsiding. Monday was spent organizing men, machines, vehicles and materials suppliers. PNG Readymixed would be one of our main suppliers, so I called on Steve, the boss, to say hello I'm back. I've known Steve since 1990, and we've had our differences, but nothing to kill for. Barry told him I would be coming back to do the job, but he wanted to see me himself before extending credit, which will be considerable once we start pouring concrete.

On Wednesday I met Tony, the SMEC (Snowy Mountains Engineering Corporation) supervisor for the project. He is a small Australian with a big voice, and even bigger opinion of himself. Lord spare us contractors from such people in positions of authority. It didn't take me long to nickname him Tony Boloney. Meanwhile I got on with organizing the job, which included the detail survey and setting out, because Barry can't afford a surveyor. The Works Dept surveyor showed me his reference pegs, which he had re-checked and set in concrete, and I took it from there myself. Theoretically Works is the main contractor, but in fact they don't do any of the work themselves. Nevertheless, claims by us for payment will be checked by SMEC and payment made to Works, who deduct their 'fees' before passing on to us. This was apparently part of the reason for the delay in signing the contract. Barry wanted a guarantee from SMEC that none of our money would 'get lost' at the Works Dept. Such things happen frequently in this country.

By the end of the second week I was very annoyed with my Project Supervisor. He is a PNG man, who served his time as carpenter, then did a course at Lae Technical College. There is no doubt in my mind he is well educated and intelligent, but his timekeeping is hopeless. Three times in ten days I've had to talk to him about having days off without good reason. In the end I told him I'm sending him back to Barry, because he is of no use to me as a part-time supervisor. He refused to go back, and hung around for the rest of the day, giving out orders. At stopping time I told him he was not to come on site tomorrow. Next morning he turned up again, so I took him aside and had a serious talk. The gist of it was that he will go back to Barry in Taraka for reassignment. He said he is the only person qualified to do the job, so he is staying, and will report the matter to SMEC and the Labour Department if I replace him with somebody less qualified. I told him I will be replacing him with somebody *more* qualified – myself. He gaped at me, but I told him I'm serious. What's more, if he doesn't go to taraka right now, I will go round the site telling all the foremen and leading hands they are not to take direction from him, thereby shaming him in public.. He went, and I am now Project manager, Surveyor and Supervisor. On the bright side, it cuts down on communications misunderstandings when you're communicating with yourself. Mind you, I am now a very busy man from dawn until well after dusk.

At the start of week 3 I had the inevitable showdown with Tony Boloney. He had taken on himself to give instruction and directions to the roadworks crew, much to the annoyance of the foreman. He is not supposed to give direct instructions to anyone, merely to supervise, inspect and report. That hasn't stopped him however, as he loves bossing people around. Since he knows very little about concreting, and absolutely nothing about stonepitched monsoon drains up to sven feet deep, he has decided to give the roadworks crew the benefit of his knowledge in their department. Though I have already christened him Tony Boloney, I think the men prefer Pain-in-the-Ass.

Anyway, there he was directing them on preparing a section of sub base, and from two hundred yards away I could see a part of it deflecting too much whenever the roller passed over it. I went for a closer look, and an area not much bigger than a kid's paddling pool was almost pure clay. I rdragged the toe of my boot around it, and told the foreman to dig it out and replace with river gravel. Up stalks Tony Boloney and says

"What are you doing? I already passed this section, if you dig it out I won't sign for it."

"That is not fit to lay base course on, it's coming out and you'll sign for it."

"Like hell I will asshole, and I'll get you thrown off the job."

He was waving his arms around, and shouting for everyone to hear. On the other hand I was deliberately keeping my voice calm and even.

"Tony, as long as I am Project Manager here, when I say it comes out, it *will* come out."

"Get stuffed."

He then started to walk away, as I told the foreman to fetch a bucket. When he did so, I asked him to get one of the labourers to fill it with material from the marked area. Tony's curiosity got the better of him.

"What the hell are you doing now asshole?"

I moved closer to him and spoke calmly

"Little man, my asshole is only a very small part of me. The rest of me is taking this sample to the Unitech laboratory for analysis *right now,* with two of my men as witnesses. We will then find out which one of us is thrown off the job."

He puffed out his chest and glared at me. For a moment I thought, even half hoped, he was going to take a swing at me in public, in the Aussie macho manner. But he turned away, saying like a petulant schoolboy

285

"Okay, dig it out, see if I care."

Round One of the Territorial Battle of the Bulls to yours truly.

The third week of the project was nearly over when a vehicle from Head Office arrived on site with an airmail letter for me. It was postmarked Johor Baru, and was from Uncle Buang. I eagerly tore it open, and was into the second sentence when I felt as if a horse kicked me in the chest.

Liz is dead.

Lightning Source UK Ltd.
Milton Keynes UK
UKOW02f2308180515

251808UK00001B/36/P